INDIA IS A ~~DEVELOPING~~ DEVELOPED COUNTRY

SHAFI SHOUKATH

notionpress.com

INDIA · SINGAPORE · MALAYSIA

ISBN

Paperback 979-8-90112-374-4
Hardcase 979-8-90112-714-8

CONTENTS

DEDICATION

To every soldier who stood guard so we could sleep in peace.

To every freedom fighter who gave their life so we could live free.

To every leader who dreamed of a nation that would stand tall.

To every farmer whose hands keep India alive and strong.

And to every dreamer who believes that India will rise,

from developing to developed.

This book is for you.

✦ ✦ ✦

AUTHOR'S NOTE

My grandfather grew up hearing that America is a developed country and India is a developing one. My father was told the same. My teachers repeated it too.

Year after year, generation after generation, we kept saying those words, *India is a developing country.*

I am writing this book with one purpose: that our children never have to repeat that line again.

This is more than a book. It is a declaration that India has started to think, believe, and act like a developed, self-reliant, and confident nation.

India has the world's youngest population, endless talent, rich resources, and the energy to lead. We already have what it takes to stand among the world's strongest nations.

So, what holds us back?

Why do we still carry the tag of "developing"?

This book is a reminder for every Indian to see the power within, to think, dream, and work for a developed India.

It is a call to pause for a moment in our busy lives and ask ourselves, *What have I done to make my country better for the next generation?*

Through these pages, we will revisit what India once was, understand why we haven't yet reached where we should be, and see what each of us can do, as citizens, entrepreneurs, professionals, and investors, to build an India that stands tall, respected, and truly developed.

Let this not remain a book. Let it be the start of a movement.

– Shafi Shoukath

✦ ✦ ✦

1

Understanding Mother India

She wakes before dawn,

with rivers that sing through her veins,

fields that rise to the sun,

and a spirit that has never known defeat.

"A nation is not built by its wealth, but by the spirit of its people."

India's strength has never rested on wealth or might. It lives in its people–in their courage, honesty, and perseverance. From those who guard its borders to those who teach its children, every act of duty and care adds to the nation's greatness.

To understand India, one must see beyond figures and frontiers. Its identity cannot be measured in numbers. It is found in action, in faith, in the will to rebuild after every setback.

India is more than land; it is an idea carried forward through time. Old in wisdom, yet alive with energy, India has seen centuries unfold and has met each change with endurance. Every age has left a mark, and every trial has revealed inner strength.

The rivers have witnessed their growth for thousands of years. The mountains have stood as witnesses to its endurance. The soil has fed both life and dreams. From the farmer tending the field to the doctor serving in a small clinic, from the artisan shaping stone to the engineer designing new cities, every citizen adds to this unending story.

The beginning was set long before history was recorded. The Indus Valley gave the world one of its earliest civilizations, organized, advanced, and deeply connected to knowledge and trade. Over time, India became a source of learning for the world. Mathematics, medicine, astronomy, literature, and philosophy found deep expression here. India taught the value of balance between intellect and compassion, thought and service.

Challenges came, as they always do. Invasions, divisions, and long years of foreign rule tested every part of this land. Yet, the belief in freedom never faded. It survived through words, through work, through sacrifice. When independence finally came, it was not the gift of others but the result of courage and unity. The tricolor that rose on that day told the world that India had reclaimed its voice.

India today stands as a symbol of perseverance. It holds together countless faiths, languages, and ways of life. Its streets are filled with effort, its classrooms with ideas, its workshops with creation. A temple, a mosque, a church, and a gurudwara can stand side by side, each teaching respect and peace.

The true wealth of India is its people, the soldier who protects, the farmer who provides, the worker who builds, the teacher who guides, the student who dares to dream. Their effort forms the foundation of progress.

India's journey continues. It has no finish line, only milestones. Each generation takes the story forward. Each citizen carries the duty to strengthen what was built before.

And as the tricolor flies high, the land speaks to every heart in one voice:

Rise. Build. Believe. The future of India begins with you.

The Birth – When Civilization Woke

Long before written history, before kings and empires, there was Bharat. A land that rose from soil and river, held together by human effort and the will to live in harmony. Around five thousand years ago, along the Sindhu and the now-silent Saraswati, a new way of life began to take form. It was a beginning that would one day grow into the soul of India.

The people who lived in this land built something far ahead of their time. The Indus Valley Civilization stands as proof of how far human hands and minds can reach when guided by order and purpose. Cities like Harappa, Mohenjo-Daro, Dholavira, and Lothal were planned with precision. Streets ran straight and wide. Drains ran under the roads, connected to every home. Wells were built at regular intervals. Public baths and storage areas stood on raised platforms. Each detail showed care for health, cleanliness, and community.

These were not rough settlements born out of survival. They were organized towns built for living well.

Houses had bathrooms with proper outlets. Drains had soak pits to filter waste before it reached the larger system. Every brick was the same size and ratio, whether it was used in Harappa or Lothal. The people believed in order, and order became their way of life.

Lothal, near the coast of Gujarat, had one of the world's first docks, connected to the sea by a channel. Dholavira had a network of water reservoirs that collected and stored rainwater through a system of channels. Harappa had granaries to store surplus grain for harder times. Mohenjo-Daro's Great Bath stood as a place for ritual, cleanliness, and reflection. These cities were built not with greed or conquest in mind, but with the intention of living in balance.

Trade flourished across this land. Archaeologists have found beads from the Indus Valley in Mesopotamia and other ancient civilizations. Seals marked with animal symbols were used for trade. Copper tools, cotton fabrics, and pottery travelled across lands and seas. Caravans moved along dusty routes, carrying not only goods but also ideas, stories, and knowledge.

The people of Bharat valued fairness and precision. They used uniform weights and measures so that trade could happen with honesty. The smallest unit of weight was the same from one town to another. This system of equality and trust laid the foundation for how India would see cooperation as a strength, not a burden.

Nature was central to their way of life. The sun, rivers, trees, and animals were treated with respect. Clay figurines of women suggest reverence for fertility and creation. Seals depict a figure seated in meditation, surrounded by animals, hinting at an early idea of harmony between human life and nature. These were not people ruled by fear of gods but guided by respect for life.

Art and creativity found a place in everyday living. Beads made of carnelian and lapis lazuli, pottery painted with simple patterns, and toys shaped like animals tell us that beauty and joy were as important as work and order. There were toys with wheels and whistles, showing that the people of the Indus Valley valued play and curiosity as much as progress.

The word "India" carries the memory of those rivers. The Persians called the Sindhu "Hindu," and the land beyond it became known as Hindustan. The Greeks called it "Indoi." To those who lived here, it was Bharat, a name drawn from King Bharata, and from the words *Bha* for light and *Rata* for devotion. Bharat means a land devoted to light and learning.

The people of ancient India measured greatness by wisdom, not by force. Their struggle was never for power, but for understanding. They studied the movement of the stars. They learned to grow crops and domesticate animals. They built with purpose. They traded with fairness. They prayed with humility. They created a culture that believed in learning and self-restraint rather than expansion and war.

They were connected to the wider world, yet distinct in spirit. From the ruins, we know that they traded with Mesopotamia, Persia, and Central Asia. Seals found in faraway lands show that Indian goods, beads, cotton, spices, and metals, were prized across continents. But along with trade came the exchange of ideas, art, and beliefs. The people of Bharat were not isolated; they were teachers and learners at the same time.

Governance during this period was organized and cooperative. There may have been rulers, but there were no grand palaces or monuments of power. The focus was on community life, on markets, homes, and public works. The use of standardized weights, planned cities, and public sanitation points to a civic system that worked efficiently without grand displays of authority.

Agriculture was the heart of the economy. Fields yielded wheat, barley, sesame, lentils, and peas. Cotton was grown, spun, and woven into cloth–the first known use of cotton in human history. Farmers built irrigation channels to draw water from the rivers. Food storage and management systems kept communities secure. Alongside farming, artisans and traders flourished. Every profession has dignity and purpose.

The Indus script remains one of history's great mysteries. Found on seals, pottery, and copper plates, it carries symbols that suggest a rich and complex language. Though it is yet to be fully understood, it stands as a reminder of how deeply the people valued knowledge and record-keeping.

As centuries passed, this civilization began to change. Rivers altered their course. The Saraswati dried up. Floods, droughts, and changing weather patterns made survival harder. People moved eastward, carrying their skills, traditions, and ideas into the Gangetic plains. The cities may have fallen silent, but their spirit travelled forward.

The influence of the Indus Valley lives on even today. The idea of cleanliness in public life, the importance of water, the respect for nature, and the value of fair trade; these lessons from the past still shape how India lives and grows. When modern India talks of smart cities, sustainable growth, and community strength, it walks on the same path once taken by the people of Harappa and Mohenjo-Daro.

The birth of civilization in Bharat was not marked by kings or wars. It was marked by knowledge, by creation, and by the desire to live in balance with the world. The story of this land's beginning reminds us that real power lies in discipline, unity, and respect for life.

When one stands among the ruins of Harappa or walks through the excavated streets of Mohenjo-Daro, there is a stillness that speaks. The bricks may be worn, but they hold the memory of a people who built with purpose, who believed that order and harmony were the highest forms of strength.

Civilization first woke here, and it did not wake with noise or conquest. It woke with thought, with effort, and with devotion. That awakening was the first light of India, a light that still burns, asking each generation a timeless question:

Will you build with the same care, the same faith, and the same love for the land that gave us all our beginning?

The Prime: The Golden Bird

To honor this nation is to see purpose and prosperity walking together, thought guiding craft, and compassion giving wealth a true direction. Across many centuries, Bharat reached a high point where scholars reasoned with patience, merchants kept fair measures, artists trained the eye for grace, and seekers turned daily life toward meaning. Hence, the world began to say *Sone Ki Chidiya*, the Golden Bird, a name earned through a rare unity of knowledge, creativity, and care that sent light outward while keeping feet firm on the soil that raised them.

Let knowledge lead your work, let kindness guide your gain, and let both serve the motherland.

A Civilisation of Knowledge

Before modern campuses fixed their gates and calendars, this land built places where learning shaped the day, where a bell gathered students and the evening lamp kept company with manuscripts, and in Nalanda, Takshashila, and Vikramashila travelers from Greece, China, Arabia, and Tibet found libraries with careful catalogues, open courtyards for debate, and refectories where teacher and pupil shared the same meal; in Nalanda alone more than ten thousand students learned with hundreds of teachers, moving through mathematics, astronomy, medicine, philosophy, literature, and statecraft, with entry earned through oral questioning and progress measured by memory, clear thinking, and service to the community.

From this ground rose minds that still steady our steps; Aryabhata set values for pi with strong precision, spoke of the Earth's rotation, and recorded procedures that shaped Indian mathematics and later enriched Arab work; Sushruta described instruments, training, and operating rooms in patient detail, repaired features with refined techniques, and treated cataracts with methods explained step by step; Panini arranged Sanskrit through the *Ashtadhyayi* as a system of rules and meta-rules that continues to guide modern linguists; Chanakya, known as Kautilya, composed the *Arthashastra*, a study of economics, administration, and strategy that treats leadership as a craft joined to foresight, ethics, and responsibility.

These achievements drew strength from a shared ethic that treated curiosity as a duty, so wisdom moved from cloister to marketplace and from palm-leaf manuscript to council hall, a theorem could guide irrigation, a verse could shape judgment, and the search for truth became a way to face the universe with respect while finding a worthy place within it.

Study hard, argue fairly, serve others, and let learning turn into action.

Trade, Industry, and Prosperity

Patriotism lives in the ledger and the workshop as much as in the song, and in cities such as Ujjain, Pataliputra, Madurai, and Varanasi that spirit took practical shape, since guild halls set standards, treasuries kept palm-leaf accounts, and workshops turned thread, metal, stone, and dye into goods for both ritual and daily use; across the long span that precedes colonial rule, India's share of the world's production has been estimated near a quarter, which signals skilled labor, steady administration, and exchange that linked districts to distant shores.

Harbors carried this movement onto open water; Lothal in Gujarat maintained a stone dock and ordered warehouses, Muziris on the Kerala coast received ships noted in the *Periplus* and in Roman letters, Calicut under the Zamorins welcomed Arab navigators and Chinese fleets, Surat handled bullion and textiles for western seas, and Masulipatnam on the Coromandel coast sent cottons toward Southeast Asia; spices, textiles, gems, and worked metals traveled outward while methods, scripts, and stories moved both ways, Roman writers complained that gold crossed the waters to pay for pepper and fine fabric, and visitors such as Megasthenes, Al-Biruni, and Ibn Battuta wrote of streets full of artisans, markets with calibrated weights, and libraries where manuscripts stood in careful rows.

Industry here paired skill with conscience; muslin drawn so fine it could pass through a ring, silk carrying motifs of region and ceremony, carpets built from patient geometry, jewelry recording lineage and vows, pottery and metalware serving kitchens, shrines, and travel; *shreni*, the guilds, trained apprentices, enforced quality, and guarded fair dealing, while *dharma* guided exchange so that revenues and donations built wells, rest houses, hospitals, schools, granaries, tanks, and canals, and port dues kept roads and causeways in repair, which turned prosperity into continuity and kept the Golden Bird in flight across generations.

Work cleanly, pay fairly, build what lasts, and let your success lift many hands.

Art, Architecture, and Culture

A nation's heart shows in stone, in song, and in story, and in these centuries art served as prayer, record, and schooling for the spirit; temples, palaces, and public halls taught the eye to seek balance, the hand to honor proportion, and the mind to stand calm before mystery, and in the caves of Ajanta and Ellora, cut from living rock, murals and sculpture held scenes of merchants and monks, rulers and mothers, reflections on life and cosmic thought standing together without quarrel; the temples of Khajuraho placed the human form beside the divine so that body and spirit could be read as partners in long work, and later the Mughal ateliers raised cities and monuments of measured beauty, with Fatehpur Sikri and its courtyards, the Taj Mahal with symmetry that feels like breath, and the Red Fort where engineering and ornament keep each other in conversation.

Music and dance rose beside stone and color; the raga system treated sound as a living order with time and mood, a path that can carry longing, peace, courage, and praise, and the classical forms of Bharatanatyam, Kathak, and Odissi told stories through gesture, footwork, and gaze, turning devotion, heroism, and love into a language that anyone can feel.

Literature thrived in many tongues; the voices of Kabir, Mirabai, Tulsidas, and Amir Khusrau crossed lines of region, language, and faith, their verses moving from courtyard to field and from scholar's chamber to soldier's march, speaking to what the human spirit seeks when it listens with courage.

In this age, art, thought, and worship shared the same table; yoga trained attention, meditation steadied breath and mind, Ayurveda held health as balance grown over seasons, and the pursuit of beauty, learning, and harmony belonged to daily life rather than a distant elite, so greatness found its measure in clear thinking, generous action, and creativity that served neighbors as faithfully as it pleased the eye.

Hold your roots, honour your craft, speak truth with grace, and let your talent serve the flag.

Spiritual and Social Harmony

The golden centuries were an age of questions of meaning beside questions of law and learning, and many paths lived together in the same towns and courts, since Hinduism, Buddhism, Jainism, and later Sikhism. It created room for dialogue, patience, and moral reflection that touched daily life as much as sacred spaces.

Rulers treated compassion as strength, and Ashoka stands clear in memory, because governance turned toward welfare, with hospitals raised for healing, trees planted for shade and soil, and grain moved with order to people who needed it most.

At the centre stood *dharma*, understood as duty joined with justice and compassion, and this idea tied families, guilds, and kingdoms into moral cohesion that outlasted any single reign.

Learning, art, and rule stayed close to spiritual practice; knowledge held a sacred charge, creativity worked as an offering to the divine, and wealth gained meaning when used for service, so a person could study as a path toward enlightenment, prosperity found its measure in the well-being of all, and the human spirit stood higher than material power.

Begin with kindness, hold fast to duty, and build something that will outlive you.

The Legacy of the Golden Bird

The Golden Bird speaks to a civilisation that held material prosperity together with moral and spiritual depth, and its gifts travel across time and sea, since this land gave zero and the decimal system, the medical wisdom of Ayurveda, the discipline of yoga, and wide philosophies that study the mind, the cosmos, and the rules that keep a society fair.

Endurance grew from ideas, culture, and ethical governance working in concert, which is why the legacy still moves among us, because mathematics from this soil shaped global science, surgical methods saved lives and trained future healers, architecture continues to inspire the eye and the hand, literature still touches the heart, and spiritual practices calm the mind and strengthen homes and halls around the world.

To understand this period is to see India as a living idea as well as a nation, a civilizational force that can nurture knowledge, compassion, and creativity on a tremendous scale, and to carry that insight forward is to choose work that honours people, policies that honour ethics, and art that honours truth.

Study with courage, serve with grace, build with care, and let your effort make the nation stronger each day.

When a nation falters, what do its children do? They stand taller, they hold the line, they remember who they are.

The Fall: Shadows Over the Golden Land

Every bright age meets an evening sky. India's golden years, too, came to a slow close, not with one fall, but through many small wounds. Power shifted, kingdoms turned against one another, and over time, the land that had once taught the world now found itself fighting to hold its ground.

The change was quiet at first. The unity that had carried the Mauryan and Gupta empires began to break apart. New rulers rose with their own dreams. Some built, some fought, and the ties that once held the country together started to fray.

Freedom in every corner brought colour to life, art, language, and music bloomed in ways unseen before. But this freedom also brought risk. Rich cities drew invaders. Trade routes that once carried silk and knowledge soon carried armies. The same openness that had connected India to the world now made her vulnerable.

Yet even when power was scattered, the pulse of the nation stayed strong. The scholar in his monastery kept teaching. The craftsman in his workshop kept creating. The poet, sitting by a lamp, still wrote of love and faith. Across villages and kingdoms, small hands held the thread of a great tradition.

India has always had this gift: to fall, to rise, and to remember. Her empires might have broken, but her spirit never learned how to bow.

The Fractures Within

The first cracks didn't come from outsiders. They began within.

The great Mauryan and Gupta empires that had once brought vast lands together started to weaken. Rulers changed, kingdoms broke away, and the map of India began to look like a patchwork of ambitions. In one region, prosperity thrived. In another, rivalry took root. Alliances were made in one season and broken in the next.

At first, this freedom gave rise to beauty. Every kingdom is built in its own style. Local art and culture found a voice of their own. Music, poetry, and craftsmanship reached new corners of the land. But the same independence that gave birth to creativity also opened doors to danger.

The wealth of India, her fertile plains, her great cities, her endless trade, drew the attention of foreign powers. The same routes that once carried merchants and travellers now brought soldiers and conquerors. Without unity, even strong kingdoms stood alone, and isolation made them easy to defeat.

Still, India's true strength has never come only from the crown or the sword. It has always lived in her people. When palaces fell, the villages kept singing. When rulers fought, the teachers kept their schools alive. When trade slowed, artisans still carved, painted, and built. Every ordinary person became a keeper of the nation's memory.

Through broken borders and lost battles, the spirit of India refused to fade. Empires came and went, but the ideas that held the country together, faith, wisdom, and kindness, continued to breathe in every home, every prayer, every song.

The Waves of Invaders/When the World Came to India

For thousands of years, this land drew the attention of distant kingdoms. From the Persian incursions in the 6th century BCE to Alexander's march across the northwest, India was seen as a realm of wealth and wisdom. Many came chasing gold or conquest; few expected to be changed by what they found.

Every wave of invasion carried its own mix of ruin and renewal. Some brought destruction, others left behind ideas, crafts, and stories that took root here. Through all of it, Bharat never lost her centre. She absorbed what could serve her, shaped it in her own way, and carried on.

In the medieval centuries came new rulers–Turkish, Afghan, and later the Mughals. The Mughal courts, in time, gave the world a language of beauty through their architecture and art. The Taj Mahal and Red Fort still stand as reminders of that vision. Persian verse met Indian rhythm, and together they gave birth to Urdu, a tongue that holds both grace and longing.

But these were also years of hardship. Raids burned villages, heavy levies drained fields, and many families were uprooted. Temples and towns were looted, yet life found a way back. Communities rebuilt what they lost. Monasteries kept their lamps lit. Artists, poets, and teachers carried on their work in smaller, quieter places when palaces fell silent.

India's endurance has never rested on the sword or the treasury. It lives in her capacity to renew, to turn pain into learning, and disruption into creation.

When freedom feels far away, strength comes from remembering who we are and what we refuse to lose.

Colonial Rule: The True Test/The Age of Struggle and Strength

The hardest test of India's spirit came with the long years of European rule. It began with merchants carrying spices and silk, and ended with an empire claiming the land itself. The British East India Company first came as a guest in the 1600s, trading under permission. Within a few generations, the guest took the host's seat. By the mid-1700s, India had become the centrepiece of Britain's global power, called their "jewel in the crown."

That crown was heavy for those who lived beneath it. The old economy, once a network of thriving local industries, was stripped apart. Goods once crafted in India now arrive from British mills. Weavers and artisans lost their looms, farmers faced crushing taxes, and famine followed bad harvests. Within a century, a civilisation that once held a quarter of the world's wealth was left with almost nothing.

The damage was not only in numbers. Divide-and-rule politics tore through the fabric of the community, setting neighbour against neighbour. Old councils that once kept local order were replaced by a distant authority. Schools began to train clerks, not thinkers. The system that had once valued wisdom was now built to serve control.

Still, something deeper held. Rebellion rose in many forms on battlefields, in classrooms, and through words that carried defiance. The uprising of 1857, though crushed, sent a message that would echo for generations: the people of this land would not live forever under another's command. Farmers, poets, teachers, and reformers began to shape a quiet revolution that could not be undone.

Freedom did not arrive as a gift. It grew through courage, through loss, through an unbroken belief that dignity could not be conquered.

Cultural and Intellectual Survival

Political power faded in many periods, yet India's culture kept its light. Scholars cared for Sanskrit, Persian, and the great family of regional tongues such as Tamil, Bengali, Marathi, Gujarati, Punjabi, and Telugu; they copied manuscripts, taught students, and kept libraries open so that memory travelled from teacher to pupil without slipping away. Poets wrote even under pressure, turning sorrow into strength and keeping literature warm in homes and courts, while artists blended native and foreign styles with care so that new forms grew without losing their roots.

Saints, teachers, and reformers reminded people of their inheritance. They called for moral courage, unity, and resilience, and they placed service at the centre of public life. In village squares and city halls, in ashrams and classrooms, they spoke of dignity and discipline, asking each person to build character as carefully as a mason lays stone.

Raja Ram Mohan Roy stood for reason and reform, arguing for education and for practices that honour human worth; he worked to open minds to modern learning while respecting India's spiritual depth. Swami Vivekananda carried India's wisdom to the world, teaching that strength and compassion walk together and that true faith brings fearlessness, self-respect, and service. Ishwar Chandra Vidyasagar fought for education for girls and for social reforms that protect families and restore fairness; he wrote simple, strong textbooks so that every child could learn.

Their work proved a central truth. Intellectual power and spiritual power can stand firm even under foreign rule. By teaching, writing, organising, and serving, they kept India's identity alive across difficult centuries, preserving languages, renewing schools, and strengthening the moral centre of society so that a new dawn could arrive on foundations already prepared.

Lessons from the Fall

The decline of India's golden age teaches us more than a list of losses. It teaches endurance. Civilisations may lose power or wealth, but they do not vanish when their people protect learning, culture, and moral values. India's fall was never final because her true strength lay deeper, in curiosity, compassion, creativity, and dharma, which held the nation steady when everything else seemed to shake.

These centuries, we learn that unity is precious, especially when it allows every belief, language, and custom to live side by side. Even the greatest of empires is weakened by greed and division. True strength lies not in armies or gold, but in knowledge and culture, treasures no conqueror can steal.

India's story reminds us that power over land may fade, but the spirit of people endures when they stay committed to learning, compassion, and self-respect. The fall was not the end. It was a lesson written in history, teaching that when hearts stay true and minds stay open, no darkness lasts forever.

The Shadow as a Teacher

Hard years came to India through invasions, fragmentation, and colonisation. These trials hurt families and towns, yet they also taught clear lessons. A nation needs resilience, fair rule, and the ability to adjust while holding to what is right. Wealth passes from hand to hand. Empires rise and fall. Wisdom, learning, and moral courage carry forward.

Even when foreign powers tried to control this land, India cared for her soul in steady ways. Classrooms kept teaching. Poets wrote and shared words that gave strength. Farmers worked their fields despite heavy burdens. Villagers protected songs, rituals, and customs so children would know who they are.

These everyday acts became seeds of renewal. They proved that a civilisation rooted in ideas and ethics stands firm through long seasons. It bends, it heals, it grows again.

The Resurrection: The Soul That Never Surrendered

Long nights can feel endless, yet morning arrives, and suffering can feel heavy, yet hope finds a way to grow. For India, that morning came on 15 August 1947, when centuries of struggle, endurance, and steadfast resistance rose into freedom.

This moment carried more than the end of foreign rule. It felt like a return to oneself, a rebirth of a great civilisation that had guarded its wisdom through storms, kept its learning alive in homes and schools, and held its faith in the dignity of every person.

The flag rose, and with it rose a promise to rebuild with patience and pride. The nation chose unity without losing its many languages and customs, chose service over anger, and chose learning as the path to a stronger future.

What began that day has asked for steady hands and brave hearts. The work has called for honesty in public life, care for the poorest, and respect for the teachers, farmers, artisans, and workers who keep the country standing.

Freedom opened a door, and the country walked through it with purpose. The soul of India had endured through every trial, and on that morning, it stood visible to the world, ready to create, ready to heal, ready to lead.

The Dawn of Freedom

India's independence grew over more than a century, through courage that lasted across seasons, through careful planning that lived in homes and ashrams and courtrooms. Through a vision carried by people who worked with their hands, taught in schools, prayed in temples and mosques, argued in debate halls, served in uniforms, and walked in long columns on dusty roads, where heat pressed on bare forearms and yet the line kept moving because the purpose felt larger than any single day's fatigue.

Leaders stood out and left marks that still guide us, with Mahatma Gandhi placing nonviolent resistance at the centre of public life so that restraint became strength in action, with Jawaharlal Nehru speaking for a future that valued science, fairness, and a modern state that would serve citizens.

Sardar Patel brought provinces and princely states into a single Union through patient negotiation and firm administration, with Bhagat Singh offering a fearless youth's sacrifice that lit many minds.

Subhas Chandra Bose summoned a hard will to fight under a national flag raised far from home soil, and with B. R. Ambedkar shaping the social promise into law so that dignity travelled from court to street and from text to life. Together, these strands formed a struggle that felt unmistakably Indian in method, purpose, and memory.

The fight answered a political need while anchouring itself in moral duty and a spiritual sense that truth carries power when it is lived every day; Gandhi's Satyagraha turned that belief into practice, as neighbours gathered for meetings, as workers chose boycott over bitterness, as families spun khadi by lamplight, as students accepted prison rather than silence, as salt pans at Dandi received the imprint of bare feet, and as petitions, marches, fasts, and songs multiplied until an empire found itself tiring against a people who would not surrender their self-respect.

When the tricolour rose over the Red Fort, it spoke of more than a constitutional change, since the moment tied villages to cities, elders to children, and memory to decision, and it honoured languages, crafts, and faiths that had survived long pressures and yet continued to teach, heal, farm, trade, study, and create.

That flag marked a turn from endurance to authorship, a declaration that India would think with clarity, care for every citizen with purpose, and step onto the world stage with its own voice steady and recognisable.

The Challenge of Rebuilding

Freedom opened the door to work that demanded steady hands and clear heads, since the country stood wide in its diversity and faced poverty, low literacy, and weak infrastructure, and the promise of independence called for action that reached schools, farms, courts, roads, and the daily lives of families who wanted dignity to move from hope to habit.

The task before the nation asked leaders and citizens to strengthen institutions, revive the economy, draw communities together, and make justice a lived reality for every person, and this meant patient effort in Parliament and panchayat, in universities and cooperatives, in factories where new machines arrived, and in villages where a clinic could change the arc of a child's life.

The Constitution of India, adopted in 1950, set out a clear charter of liberty, equality, fraternity, and justice, and it drew from centuries of Indian reflection while placing modern democratic ideals at the centre of public life; for the first time in formal law, the Republic guaranteed rights to every citizen irrespective of caste, gender, or religion, a civilisational step that turned ancient debates on duty and fairness into a living framework that courts could uphold and children could learn.

Economic reconstruction moved alongside this moral and legal foundation, with national plans to modernise agriculture, industry, and infrastructure, and with investment flowing to dams, research institutions, public sector undertakings, and transport that tied regions to markets and people to opportunity.

The Green Revolution raised yields through better seeds, irrigation, and scientific practice, and a country that had once struggled to feed itself grew secure in grain and learned to manage scarcity with knowledge rather than fear; the White Revolution expanded dairying through cooperatives that placed small producers at the heart of the value chain, and morning milk from countless villages began to travel to towns and cities with efficiency and fairness, lifting incomes while improving nutrition for children and elders.

Through these choices, the Republic affirmed self-reliance with inclusion, science with social purpose, and growth with rights, and the work of rebuilding became a shared duty, where every artisan, teacher, farmer, engineer, and judge could see their efforts reflected in the nation's broader rise.

Science, Technology, and Global Presence

Renewal meant reclaiming India's seat at the table of knowledge and invention, as scientists, engineers, and scholars set to work with a patience born of study and a confidence shaped by centuries of enquiry, so the nation's intellectual legacy gathered strength in laboratories, observatories, classrooms, and design studios that trained hands and minds for service at scale.

- Aryabhata, the first Indian satellite, signalled a clear return to space science with a spirit that honoured the country's mathematical heritage while pointing new students toward the sky, and the launch marked the beginning of a steady climb in capability that linked classroom effort to orbiting hardware.
- The Indian Space Research Organisation carried that intent further with missions to the Moon and Mars, and these ventures proved that careful

planning, disciplined teams, and public trust could send Indian-built craft across deep space, inspiring young readers who might one day write code for guidance systems or test components on clean-room benches.

- Advances in medicine, digital technology, and renewable energy showed how classical insight and modern research can stand together, as Ayurveda-informed studies met rigorous clinical methods, as engineers built affordable devices for diagnosis and care, and as energy programmes brought solar parks and decentralised solutions that let villages light schools and power small enterprises.

This renewal leaned on India's own creative centre rather than imitation, applying knowledge for human welfare, building tools that lower cost without lowering standards, and proving that a civilisation confident in its memory and open in its science can speak to the world with results that matter in daily life.

Understood. Here's a more grounded, people-first rewrite in British English, with simple language, longer flowing sentences, and plenty of paragraph breaks. I've kept the core ideas and trimmed anything that might feel formulaic.

Cultural Renaissance

Freedom opened doors for everyday expression, in living rooms and reading circles, in school assemblies and open grounds, where literature, music, dance, and painting carried the confidence of a country learning to speak in its many voices while holding a shared centre.

Writers such as R. K. Narayan, Mulk Raj Anand, and Rabindranath Tagore stayed present in classrooms and in home libraries, where a short story could send a reader back to the streets of Malgudi, where a novel could show the weight of injustice on a young worker, and where a poem could steady a conscience with simple lines that stayed in memory; these works encouraged readers to think with care, to notice the lives around them, and to choose fairness without waiting for permission.

Cinema and theatre reached large audiences in towns and cities, in single-screen halls with hand-painted posters and in touring productions that set up lights and curtains for a weekend run, while classical forms such as Bharatanatyam, Kathak, Odissi, Kuchipudi, and Kathakali grew through patient training and public support, and Hindustani and Carnatic traditions drew students to practise scales, compositions, and improvisations until craft felt natural and stage presence felt earned; from studios in Bombay, Chennai, and Kolkata to small cultural academies in district centres, the arts offered learning, pride, and honest entertainment at the same time.

Social reform moved with this creative energy, with determined steps to end untouchability in public life, to widen opportunity for women through education and work, and to bring schooling to children who had long stood outside the gates, and progress showed up in legal protections, in scholarships that helped a first-generation learner stay enrolled, in self-help groups that built confidence and savings, and in campaigns that tied dignity to everyday practice.

India's renewal rested on morality and human dignity alongside roads, grids, and factories, since a country grows well when its artists can speak freely, when its laws defend the weak, and when its teachers help a child read with understanding, and this is how culture strengthened unity without losing variety, giving people a sense that their stories and songs belonged in the national conversation.

The Spirit of Unity in Diversity

One of India's finest achievements after independence has been the steady keeping of unity across a land that holds many languages, faiths, and customs, with twenty-two official languages and countless dialects spoken in homes and marketplaces, and with ways of worship and ways of living that carry long memory while meeting daily needs in cities, towns, and villages.

The idea of unity in diversity moved from slogan to practice as festivals, rituals, and cultural traditions that had survived storms across centuries began to be marked across the nation, and people found in one another's celebrations a chance to share food, music, stories, and work, which in time built a sense of belonging that felt stronger than any single marker of difference.

Communities that had once stood apart for historical, religious, or regional reasons learned cooperation through school committees, local councils, cooperatives, service groups, sports, and shared markets, and tolerance grew into respect when neighbours saw that strength increases when differences are held with care, since a large country stands taller when each voice finds room without drowning the others.

India Today: A Nation of Dreams and Challenges

India today carries old wisdom and new energy in the same breath, with ancient heritage and modern ambition living side by side, with rural depth and urban scale shaping policy and enterprise, with tradition offering guidance while innovation opens fresh doors in science, arts, governance, and business.

Real challenges remain in poverty, inequality, climate stress, and tense neighbourhoods, yet the country also holds immense capacity, since a young and energetic population of more than 1.4 billion people works within the world's fifth-largest economy, and this size, skill, and will now place India in a position to shape global conversations in trade, technology, health, education, culture, and ideas.

India's renewal can be seen in simple scenes that carry a larger meaning:

- A farmer in Punjab uses modern irrigation and soil testing while keeping practices learnt from elders, so that yield, water care, and respect for land move together.
- An engineer in Bengaluru building software that connects people across continents while holding to the values of fairness, frugality, and service that were taught at home and school.
- Children in remote villages walk into classrooms built through government plans and community effort, where a library corner and a reliable meal turn attendance into learning and learning into confidence.

This rise is political and economic, and it is also spiritual, moral, and intellectual, because a civilisation grows strong when knowledge serves dignity, when policy protects the weak, when science and ethics travel together, and when millions of ordinary lives gain the freedom to study, to work, to create, and to care for one another with pride.

The Call to Her Children

Mother India's story continues in ordinary places where life is made and mended, in a classroom that starts the day with a prayer and a timetable, in a ward where a nurse changes a dressing and eases a worry, in a workshop where a fitter sets a machine right, and in a field where careful hands guide seed and water with patience while clouds roll past and seasons turn.

She asks for remembrance more than rescue, for citizens who know their names and inheritances, who carry pride with humility, and who place effort where it counts, in study that sharpens judgement, in craft that serves neighbours, in law kept with courage, and in the steady raising of children who read well, think clearly, and act with kindness even when nobody is watching.

Her rise offers a lesson the world can hear. A nation gains stature through the character of its people, through fair dealing, through care shown to elders and to those at the margin, through the strength to speak truth in small rooms as well as in great halls, and through a long view that holds faith with memory while planning for the years ahead. India shows that hard seasons may press upon a society, yet patience joined with learning and public spirit can renew the ground under our feet.

The tricolour that moves in the wind carries more than a date from the past; it holds a pledge to keep learning, to create with skill, to serve with compassion, and to endure with grace, and it calls every citizen to add a line to this larger story through daily work in classrooms, clinics, farms, courts, laboratories, studios, and start-ups, where care for people and care for excellence stand side by side and where conscience keeps ambition honest.

The golden bird rises when courage, inventiveness, and moral clarity guide effort in every lane, when prosperity walks with dignity, when success shows in wider opportunity, in clean air and safe water, in streets that welcome all, and in minds that stay curious from youth to old age.

How do we truly measure development, not only in numbers and markets, but in the growth of the human spirit and shared purpose?

✦ ✦ ✦

2

UNDERSTANDING DEVELOPMENT

"Development is freedom." – Amartya Sen

India stands ready to turn possibility into proof. The task is clear. Define development in full, measure it honestly, and pursue it with courage.

Skylines, expressways, and factories matter. Yet the heart of development lives in people. It lives in a child who learns well, a patient who receives timely care, a farmer who earns steadily, a worker who returns home with dignity, a young founder who solves a real problem and creates jobs. True progress strengthens the base of life. Equality. Fair opportunity. Knowledge. Trust.

Two lessons from our times make the point.

- South Africa shows strong airports, banks, and tall buildings, yet inequality remains severe, and safety and employment need steady work.

- Bhutan runs with modest infrastructure in many districts, yet places well-being, fairness, and nature at the centre of public choice.

These mirrors teach that development has many parts. Income, health, learning, freedom, safety, decent work, and care for rivers, soil, and air. Some parts can be counted. Some are felt in daily life. The full picture needs both.

India brings strengths that few nations hold. Population of more than 1.4 billion. Median age in the late twenties. Over 850 million internet users. A digital payments rail that clears billions of UPI transactions each month and brings a street vendor and a global firm onto the same platform. Jan Dhan has opened hundreds of millions of bank accounts and tied benefits to identity and mobile.

Electricity reaches nearly every household. LPG connections have expanded to rural kitchens. Clean water and toilets have reached crores of homes in the past decade. Renewable capacity has passed a major mark and grows each year with solar parks, rooftop systems, and wind corridors. These are foundations that lift daily life.

Facts also remind us where we must move faster. Life expectancy sits a little above 70 years. The Human Development Index still leaves room to climb. Learning outcomes in early grades need a strong push. Women's labour-force participation can rise much higher. Air quality in several cities demands bold action. Farmers in rain-fed regions still face high risk from weather swings. The work ahead is known and actionable.

So, What is Development for India?

- Every child reads fluently by Class 3, reaches Class 10 with strong maths and science, and finishes school healthy and confident.

- Every mother reaches a clinic with trained staff, medicines, and reliable power.
- Every village has piped water, a quality school, a good road to the nearest market, and a digital link that works.
- Every city adds buses, footpaths, and drains before it adds cars, while treating water and cleaning air.
- Every youth leaves school or college with employable skills and a first rung of work within reach.
- Every small business can register, pay, borrow, and sell online without friction.
- Every farmer has soil information, irrigation support, storage, insurance, and fair market access.
- Every office of the state answers with transparency, time-bound service, and audited outcomes.

Plans and budgets make these outcomes possible. Values give them direction. Technology helps when it serves people. Digital public goods have already changed daily life. UPI moved cash to the phone. DigiLocker moved paper to secure cloud storage. Direct transfers moved benefits to the person who earned them. The next step is depth. Learning platforms that lift outcomes, health records that cut delay, crop advisories that save water, and skilling that leads to real jobs.

Hard truths deserve a firm look and decisive answers.

Inequality of access to quality education calls for early-years nutrition, teacher support, and measurement that guides teaching.

Health gaps call for primary care first, then referral clarity, then hospital capacity, along with more local production of drugs and equipment.

Urban stress calls for clean buses, last-mile links, stormwater systems, safe rental housing, and land-use that brings jobs and homes closer.

Rural incomes call for irrigation where sound, micro-irrigation where water is scarce, producer collectives, food processing, and storage at scale.

Jobs at scale call for logistics parks, power reliability, compliance that is simple and stable, and export-ready clusters for textiles, electronics, autos, chemicals and food.

Climate risk calls for solar on every roof that can hold it, wind where corridors allow, pumped hydro and batteries for balance, and a clear local plan for heat, flood, and drought in every district.

Progress must be measured with care. GDP per capita matters. So do jobs created, women in the workforce, child stunting reduced, learning scores improved, median time to start a firm, median time to resolve a court case, air-quality days gained, water bodies revived, and corruption cases deterred by design. What gets measured gets managed. What gets shared with citizens gets managed better.

The spirit needed is clear. Courage to face data. Patience to stay the course. Pride in work done well. Fairness in who benefits. Unity in purpose across party and state lines. The world competes in science, design, and markets. India's edge rests in its people. Students who write code and build hardware. Farmers who renew soil and water. Scientists who reach the moon and map our own seas and skies. Artisans who turn heritage into global demand. Nurses, teachers, soldiers, and officers who carry daily duties without fanfare. When this energy is aligned with clear outcomes, the rise becomes visible and durable.

Let this be our stance.

Teach every child well.

Heal every family well.

Build every road and pipe well.

Protect every river well.

Register, tax, and serve every enterprise well.

Judge every dispute well and in time.

Reward integrity, skill, and effort at every level.

Development is freedom in practice. Freedom from hunger and fear. Freedom to learn and work. Freedom to start and grow. Freedom to breathe clean air and drink safe water. Freedom to dream beyond the limits of the last generation.

India stands ready. The figures tell a story of momentum. The gaps tell us where to aim next. The choice now is simple to state and strong to pursue. Move from promise to proof, from pilot to scale, from short bursts to steady gains.

The next generation is watching. Let them see a nation wide awake.

What Is Development?

"Development is not the accumulation of wealth, nor the expansion of cities, nor the power of nations. Development is the awakening of human potential, the flourishing of life itself."

True progress begins with people. It cannot be measured by the height of buildings or the length of highways alone. Development is the strength of a society to uplift every life, to open doors where once there were walls, and to make every citizen feel part of the nation's journey.

The People Behind Progress

Development grows when a young student in Rajasthan can study without fear, when a farmer in Punjab earns fairly for his labour, when a nurse in a small clinic in Odisha has medicine and light to treat her patients, and when a small business owner in Surat can expand without red tape. These stories, repeated across millions of homes, form the real face of progress.

It is the freedom to think, to learn, to work, and to live with dignity. When a nation removes barriers that hold people back, social, economic, or systemic, its true potential begins to unfold.

Growth Beyond Numbers

Economic growth adds strength, but alone it cannot complete the story. A nation may record a high GDP and yet struggle with hunger, poor health, or unsafe streets. Development gains meaning only when prosperity touches every home.

South Africa shows the limits of growth that leaves gaps. Cities like Johannesburg and Cape Town display wealth, yet inequality runs deep. At the other end, Bhutan proves that human well-being matters as much as income. It values happiness, equality, and the environment. Yet, it too needs wider opportunities for education and employment. Both examples show that development is balanced, between progress and fairness, between economy and human well-being.

What We Build, and What We Become

Bridges, roads, schools, and hospitals are vital. They carry goods and people, save time, and make life easier. Yet the inner growth of a nation is built on trust, ethics, and equal opportunity. If corruption thrives, if schools fail to teach, if citizens lose faith in institutions, even the best infrastructure stands empty of meaning.

Japan proved this after the devastation of 1945. The country rose from ruins by investing in education, discipline, and technology. Singapore followed a similar path, strengthening its people as much as its systems. Their examples show that progress built on integrity and skill can outlast every crisis.

Preparing for The Future

Development has to look ahead. Climate change, shrinking resources, and rapid urbanization demand foresight. Growth that damages air, water, and soil destroys its own foundation.

The story of the Aral Sea is a stark reminder. Once the lifeline of Central Asia, it vanished due to reckless irrigation. Livelihoods were lost, and the environment collapsed. Across the world, cities like Delhi, Beijing, and Mexico City face the same warning. Economic expansion without balance will always be fragile.

India's growth must secure both prosperity and sustainability. Solar and wind energy now reach new regions. Rural homes are gaining access to clean water and electricity. New technologies connect citizens to government and markets. These changes show what progress can look like when guided by both purpose and care.

The Measure of a Developed Nation

At its core, development measures the health of the human spirit. It asks if people are free to dream, to work, and to live with dignity.

A truly developed India will be one where every child learns well, every worker feels secure, every woman walks without fear, every farmer earns fairly, and every elder is treated with respect. It will be a country that grows in wealth, but also in empathy, where innovation uplifts rather than divides, and where progress brings both comfort and character.

Real development is a steady rise in the quality of life, a rise that can be seen in cleaner air, better schools, safer homes, and hearts full of hope. It is the renewal of a nation's promise to its people that no one will be left behind in the journey toward a brighter, more human future.

"The strength of a nation lies in how it uplifts its weakest citizen." – Mahatma Gandhi

To see development clearly, one must look at it from every direction. It cannot be contained in a single figure or a single measure. Progress touches every part of national life, the economy, society, governance, and the very quality of daily living. Each of these threads must move together, or the picture remains incomplete.

Economic Progress

Economic growth is the engine that powers every other goal. It shows in how much a nation produces, how many jobs it creates, and how well people live. Gross Domestic Product, or GDP, tells us the size of the economy, but it does not reveal how that wealth is shared.

India has seen remarkable economic progress in recent decades. From a GDP of 300 billion dollars in 1990, the economy now stands at over 3.5 trillion. The services sector contributes nearly 55 percent, manufacturing adds strength to exports, and agriculture still provides work to nearly half the population. Yet, challenges remain. Income inequality has widened, and rural wages have grown unevenly. True economic growth must ensure that prosperity reaches those who till the soil, build the cities, and keep the engines running.

When every citizen finds a fair chance to earn and save, when small businesses can grow without fear of failure, when farmers can access markets and credit, the economy becomes a living force, one that creates stability and pride.

Social Progress

No country can be called developed if its people suffer hunger, ill health, or ignorance. Social development is the measure of human well-being. It begins with access to education, healthcare, equality, and safety.

India has made steady strides. Literacy has reached nearly 80 percent, life expectancy has crossed 70 years, and maternal and child health indicators have improved. Yet gaps remain, between rural and urban, between men and women, and between privilege and poverty. A developed nation must bridge these gaps through quality schooling, nutrition, and skill-building for every child.

The promise of education is not in classrooms alone, but in what it gives back: the ability to think freely, to create, to solve problems, and to build a better society. When health, learning, and opportunity work together, the country's social foundation becomes strong enough to hold any storm.

Infrastructure and Technology

Bridges, ports, railways, and power grids are the arteries of a nation. They connect people and ideas. Without them, progress stays confined to a few pockets.

India's roads now stretch over six million kilometres, and the Golden Quadrilateral links major cities with speed and trade. Railway modernization, affordable air travel, and expanding metros have changed how people move. Digital connectivity has linked citizens to government services, banking, and healthcare. India's space program, the success of Chandrayaan, and the rise of its IT industry have proved that technology can lift both aspiration and confidence.

The next step is integration, an infrastructure that serves both the economy and ecology. Roads lined with solar lights, cities planned with green zones, villages powered by renewable energy, and digital tools that simplify life for every citizen. When technology uplifts people instead of overwhelming them, it becomes a true instrument of progress.

Governance and Institutions

Strong governance gives life to every policy. A nation may have wealth, but without fairness and integrity, it cannot sustain it. Governance is the bridge between vision and result.

Transparent systems, accountable leaders, and efficient institutions create an environment of trust. When laws are fair, when justice moves without delay, when corruption finds no shelter, citizens gain confidence in their nation. India's Aadhaar system, Jan Dhan accounts, and Direct Benefit Transfers have shown how technology and governance can work together to deliver support directly to the people.

Yet the deeper task remains, to make every government office a place of service, not fear; to ensure that power serves, not rules. Development thrives when institutions protect the weak, reward the hardworking, and give every citizen a sense of belonging in the national story.

Quality of Life and Harmony

At its peak, progress is measured in peace, in how people live, work, and dream. Development is meaningful when citizens breathe clean air, drink safe water, walk safe streets, and spend time with family without anxiety.

India's diversity is its strength, but it requires constant care. True harmony comes when faiths, languages, and regions grow together without one overshadowing another. Cities must plan for green spaces as they rise; villages must retain community bonds even as they modernize. Cultural heritage, music, and art carry the soul of India; they remind us that progress has meaning only when it uplifts life, not erases it.

The quality of life is the bridge between economic success and national character. It is what turns growth into happiness, and prosperity into peace.

Lessons from India and The World

Across India, progress wears many faces. In a village in Tamil Nadu, solar pumps and rainwater harvesting have doubled crop yields. In Kerala, healthcare networks reach the remotest hamlets. In Gujarat, roads and logistics hubs have powered small industries. These examples prove that when policy meets purpose, transformation follows.

Around the world, other nations show the same truth. Japan and South Korea rebuilt from ruin through education, innovation, and discipline. The Nordic countries pair prosperity with equality and trust. Bhutan measures success in human happiness, reminding us that progress must serve the heart as well as the hand.

Each story offers lessons, but India's path must be its own, one that reflects its values, its culture, and its conscience.

India's Distinct Path

India's wealth has never rested on conquest. It has grown from ideas, trade, and cooperation. From the invention of zero to the science of Ayurveda, from the Silk Route to the temples of learning at Nalanda and Takshashila, India has shown that knowledge and ethics can walk together. Prosperity guided by dharma, the principle that wealth must serve welfare, remains the finest model for our times.

Today, India's challenge is to apply those same principles in a modern context, an economy that grows fast yet includes all, governance that protects and empowers, and innovation that uplifts lives while respecting nature.

Development as Awakening

True development is the steady rise of a nation's spirit. It is not a race against others, but a promise to oneself. It is the awakening of every citizen's potential, from the farmer who feeds the nation, to the engineer who builds its future, to the artist who preserves its soul.

India's progress will gain strength when knowledge meets compassion, when growth carries responsibility, and when every citizen feels that the nation's victory is their own.

The journey of development continues, from economic power to human progress, from growth to purpose, from success to significance.

Can India now rise as a model of development that inspires the world, a nation where progress and humanity walk side by side?

✦ ✦ ✦

3

India's Wealth

What if India's true wealth has never been measured, not in gold, land, or GDP, but in the untapped potential of its people?

When people measure a nation, they often begin with totals and charts, with GDP, trade balances, and coins counted in neat columns, yet numbers cannot hold the full story of strength because the life of a country also rests in the talent, feeling, and drive of its people. India, with old civilisations, generous natural gifts, and a cultural heritage that still guides daily life, shows how wide the idea of wealth can be. Rivers, minerals, wind and sun bring power and promise, yet the pulse that carries the nation forward lies in human ingenuity, resilience, and clear ambition.

Across the years, comparisons with other countries have been common, growth rates placed side by side and factories or labs weighed against foreign examples, although this habit can hide the riches already present. Progress begins when attention turns to what stands ready to be used: fertile plains, mountains rich in ore, great river systems, a young population, and knowledge collected over centuries. The question is less a contest with distant rivals and more a test of will and organisation at home, where resources can be gathered, refined, and used with purpose.

India's story ties wealth to creation and exchange. Many powers built fortunes through conquest or control, while India's strength has flowed from making, trading, teaching, and learning, carried by an ethic that prizes self-reliance, creativity, and care for future generations. This gives a path where growth stays fair and durable, where prosperity spreads and lasts.

To see potential clearly, wealth must be read in the widest sense. Soil, water, minerals, and energy form the base for farms and industry, and human skill turns that base into food, goods, and services. India's age profile brings a special chance, since the country stands among the youngest large economies on Earth, and energy, creativity, and ambition can move invention, enterprise, and leadership forward, provided education, training, and meaningful work receive steady investment.

The ledger also includes intellectual and cultural capital. Mathematics, astronomy, medicine, literature, and philosophy from this land shaped civilisations far beyond its shores, and in our time information technology, space research, and biotechnology show that the capacity to build and inspire remains strong. Geography adds further strength. Snow peaks in the north, warm coasts in the south, wide plains, and great deserts together support agriculture, energy, tourism, health services, and knowledge industries, while a skilled workforce ties these fields into one effort.

This walks through the many faces of Indian wealth: people, natural resources, ideas, culture, finance, and technology. Each part shows what stands today and what can follow when effort, policy, and investment align. The larger story is a nation waking to its full measure, building prosperity that is sustainable, ethical, and welcoming to all.

Wealth is more than production, exports, or consumption. It also lives in a promise that every citizen can contribute and rise with others. The future on offer here blends economic strength with social, cultural, and scientific advances, setting a model that many will study. The moment suits action. By focusing on what already exists and nurturing it with clear vision and careful planning, India can share a definition of wealth measured in strength, knowledge, and spirit, not coins alone.

Human Capital: India's Greatest Asset

Farms, factories, minerals, and power lines frame growth, while people set direction and speed. Skill, creativity, knowledge, and resilience light the path. India holds a rare advantage here. With one of the largest and youngest populations in the world, the nation can convert a demographic dividend into leadership in innovation, productivity, and influence.

Demographic Advantage

More than sixty-five per cent of the population stands under thirty-five, which brings decades of active labour ahead, and only around one in ten is above sixty, a profile very different from ageing societies such as Japan, Germany, or Italy. A young population secures a long supply of labour and sparks new firms, new ideas, and healthy demand for goods and services. Countries with older profiles must push automation and expand care systems to balance shrinking workforces, while India can draw on human energy and creativity to enlarge its economy.

The gains are large, yet they do not arrive by themselves. Education, public health, and job creation must move in step. Without this, the dividend can fade into frustration and waste. Using human capital well is therefore a national duty as much as an economic aim.

Workforce Potential and Employment

The workforce is vast and underused. Each year brings millions of young entrants, though many lack the precise skills that modern industries seek. Gaps in training, uneven quality in schools and colleges, and regional differences slow absorption into high-value work. Estimates show that training and employing the young cohort at scale could add two to three trillion dollars to national output across the next two decades, lifting growth and widening India's role abroad.

Four fields carry special promise:

1. **Technology and IT services.** India already leads in outsourcing and software services. With deeper work in artificial intelligence, machine learning, cyber security, and data analytics, the country can host next-generation platforms and products.
2. **Manufacturing.** Programmes such as "Make in India" aim to improve logistics, infrastructure, and labour productivity. Skilled workers double efficiency, expand exports, and create jobs across ancillary sectors.

3. **Agriculture and rural employment.** Large shares of the population still work on farms. Mechanisation, precision agriculture, and digital supply chains raise yields and incomes and open non-farm roles in storage, processing, and logistics.
4. **Entrepreneurship and startups.** A young, ambitious builder class is solving local problems in health, finance, energy, and technology. These firms add direct jobs and many more in supply networks.

Investment in these areas ensures that the workforce adds real weight to growth and holds its own in global competition.

Education and Skill Development

Education anchors human capital. Recent decades have brought higher literacy, strong expansion in higher education, and new attention to vocational training. By 2023, literacy stood near seventy-seven per cent, with cities ahead of rural districts; enrolment in higher education crossed thirty-eight million, yet questions remain on quality and employability; many graduates still miss the benchmarks that employers set.

The answer is targeted effort across formal and vocational tracks, with a clear eye on global standards. India needs wider programmes in STEM, artificial intelligence, robotics, biotechnology, renewable energy, and health technology. Lifelong learning must become common, since industries evolve quickly.

Bridges between learning and work are vital. Curricula should match industry needs, practical training should sit within degrees, and partnerships with leading institutions worldwide should raise both skill and confidence. An educated, adaptable, globally competitive workforce can turn a young age profile into steady, long-term growth.

Comparative Advantage

Human capital gives India a strategic edge. The nation holds the largest cohort of young people anywhere, which can outpace older economies in productivity and invention when backed by training and fair opportunity.

Workforce comparison at a glance

Country	Workforce size (million)	Youth share (<35)	Innovation potential	Challenges
India	520	65%	High, underused	Skills mismatch; uneven R&D investment
USA	165	45%	High in research and design	Ageing workforce; high cost of innovation
China	780	55%	Strong in manufacturing	Skills aligned to state priorities
Germany	45	28%	Engineering focus	Slow adoption in some digital areas

Scale turns into strength when education, skills, and employment creation grow together.

Harnessing human capital for global leadership

Full use of people power changes the map across sectors:

1. **Technology hub:** Investment in AI, blockchain, biotechnology, and advanced research can seed world-class firms, strong patent portfolios, and global talent inflows.
2. **Industrial strength:** Skilled labour raises output and quality, helping India export a wider set of goods at better prices.
3. **Global education hub:** Welcoming international students brings revenue and builds an exchange of ideas that lasts for decades.
4. **Entrepreneurial ecosystem:** Startups create direct and indirect jobs while solving Indian conditions at Indian price points.
5. **Health and wellness leadership:** A trained workforce expands medical care, biotech research, Ayurveda and wellness services, and attracts patients and travellers.

The effects run beyond GDP: technological independence grows, society gains stability, global standing rises, and quality of life improves.

Challenges to Maximising Human Capital

Barriers remain clear:

1. **Skills mismatch:** Many graduates miss industry standards, which leads to underemployment.
2. **Regional disparity:** Urban centres enjoy better training and jobs; rural areas lag.
3. **Quality concerns:** Enrolment has grown while learning outcomes vary widely.
4. **Healthcare gaps:** Healthy citizens work better; weak infrastructure lowers productivity.
5. **Social barriers:** Gender inequality, caste bias, and restrictive norms hold back many.

Government, private enterprise, and civil society must act together to remove these obstacles.

People are India's greatest store of strength. With the world's largest young cohort, the nation can move into a position of lasting influence. Investment in education, skills, health, and meaningful work turns a demographic window into durable growth. On this basis, agriculture, industry, knowledge fields, tourism, and invention can rise together.

Natural gifts matter, yet the decisive force is human energy, talent, and spirit. When the potential of the young is unlocked with care and discipline, inclusive growth follows, competitiveness deepens, and prosperity endures.

Youth and ageing profile

Country	Youth population (<35)	Ageing population (>60)	Workforce note
India	65%	10%	Large untapped potential
Japan	25%	33%	Shrinking workforce
Germany	28%	27%	High dependency ratio
Italy	24%	28%	Ageing society

Workforce pathways and skills

Sector	Current employment (million)	Potential employment (million)	Key skill requirements
IT and technology	4	10	Coding; AI; data analysis
Manufacturing	50	80	Engineering; automation
Agriculture and allied	120	90	Modern farming: supply chain
Startups and entrepreneurship	1	15	Business management; innovation
Services and tourism	15	40	Hospitality; healthcare; languages

Education focus and GDP impact

Education & skill area	Current enrolment (million)	Future target (million)	Potential impact on GDP (USD billion)
STEM	8	20	500
Vocational and technical training	5	25	300
Healthcare and life sciences	2	10	200
Entrepreneurship and innovation	0.5	5	400

Sector contributions from human capital

Potential contribution	Estimated GDP impact (USD trillion)	Employment (million)
Technology and IT	1.0	10
Manufacturing and industry	0.8	25
Education and research	0.5	5
Startups and entrepreneurship	0.7	15
Healthcare and wellness	0.3	5

Agriculture: The Foundation of Growth

Agriculture has carried India through centuries. From the plains of the Ganga and the Brahmaputra to the great deltas in the South, fields have fed households, shaped festivals, and anchored trade. Long before the age of machines, ships left Indian ports with grain, spice, cotton, and sugar. That story did not end with the rise of services and technology. It evolved. Agriculture still supports livelihoods at scale and steadies the nation in years of uncertainty.

A clear picture helps. **Around 45.8% of workers were employed in agriculture and allied activities in 2022-23**, according to India's official labour survey. **Agriculture's share in Gross Value Added stood at 18.3% in 2022-23**. Foodgrain output set new records, and horticulture volumes surpassed foodgrains. Exports crossed the fifty-billion-dollar mark in FY23. These are the bones of a living system that feeds 1.4 billion and supplies raw material to industry.

India's agricultural heritage and evolution

The roots run deep. Irrigation know-how appears in the Indus Valley record. Over the centuries, farmers domesticated diverse crops and traded across Asia, Africa, and Europe. After Independence, the country chose self-sufficiency. The **Green Revolution** brought high-yield seed varieties, irrigation, and fertilisers to the field. Grain queues gave way to buffer stocks. The work is not finished. Fragmented holdings, soil fatigue, water stress, and uneven adoption of modern methods still hold yields back in parts of the country. A new push centred on sustainability, science, and value addition can lift both productivity and incomes.

The present landscape

Diversity is India's strength. Rice dominates in the East and South, wheat in the North, pulses across the Deccan, and spice and horticulture clusters thrive in the West and South. India now posts **record foodgrain output** and an **all-time high in sugarcane**, while horticulture outstrips cereals on tonnage.

India's latest production snapshot (official estimates)

Category	2022-23 estimate	Notes
Foodgrains	**330.5 million tonnes**	Third Advance Estimates, Ministry of Agriculture.
Rice	**135.5 million tonnes**	Record.
Wheat	**112.7 million tonnes**	Record.
Maize	**35.9 million tonnes**	Record.
Pulses	**27.5 million tonnes**	Gram 13.5; moong 3.7.
Oilseeds	**41.0 million tonnes**	Soybean 14.98; rapeseed-mustard 12.49.
Sugarcane	**494.2 million tonnes**	Record.
Cotton	**34.3 lakh bales (170 kg)**	Bales as per the official unit.
Horticulture (fruits, vegetables, etc.)	**-352-355 million tonnes**	Second to final estimates for 2022-23. India is the world's No. 2 producer of fruits and vegetables by volume.

India's position in many global commodity tables is strong. The country ranks among the top producers of rice, wheat, sugarcane, cotton, pulses, and a wide range of fruits and vegetables. Horticulture volumes continue to edge higher with better seed, protected cultivation, and post-harvest handling.

Room to grow: irrigation expansion, precision agronomy, climate-smart seed, storage, and logistics can still raise output and farm-gate value. Multiple studies and field pilots show double-digit gains when water, nutrients, and timing are managed with data. The opportunity is not theoretical; it is practical and visible, district by district.

The constraints we must tackle

Small plots, rainfall dependence, post-harvest loss, income volatility, and resource stress show up across states. **Nearly half of the cultivated land still relies on monsoon rain**, which magnifies weather risk. Post-harvest loss continues where storage and cold chain are thin. Groundwater and soil health need careful stewardship in pockets of intensive cultivation. These are not reasons for despair. They are targets for investment and policy.

Structural challenges and practical responses

Challenge	What it looks like on the ground	Practical response
Small and fragmented holdings	Mechanisation and scale efficiencies are harder to realise	Promote Farmer-Producer Organisations, shared services, and custom-hiring centres
Rainfall dependence	Yield swings with monsoon spread and timing	Expand micro-irrigation, recharge, and watershed work; service-based irrigation markets

Post-harvest loss	Limited cold rooms, grading, and reefer links	Build pack-houses, cold chain, and rural logistics with viability gap support
Price and income volatility	Thin market access and uneven information	e-NAM reach, quality grading, warehouse receipts, better MSP operations, where notified
Soil and water stress	Input overuse, falling water tables in hotspots	Soil health cards, balanced nutrients, millets and pulses in rotations, deficit irrigation

(General framing; complements crop-wise programmes already in place.)

Technology and innovation at the farm-edge

Drones now scout fields. Sensors flag moisture and disease early. Farm apps match input use to weather. Market platforms shorten the distance between farmer and buyer. **India hosts a large and rising agritech base**. One independent analysis notes **nearly 2,800 agritech startups recognised by Startup India as of December 2023**, with many using AI, remote sensing, and traceability tools.

Why this matters: better timing, lower waste, and transparent pricing protect margins for smallholders. Public digital rails and private innovation together can move outcomes at scale.

Exports and global presence

Agricultural exports reached about USD 53.1 billion in 2022-23, with APEDA-linked products contributing around half the value. In 2023–24, exports hovered near **USD 50 billion** as temporary curbs on staples balanced domestic prices, while other categories such as basmati, fruits, vegetables, and processed foods grew.

Where the world meets Indian produce

Theme	Current footing	Key step to move up the value curve
Rice, spices, and marine products	Consistent top-tier exporter by value	Brand India by origin, residue-free certification, and GI-led positioning
Fruits and vegetables	Rising fresh and processed volumes	Cold-chain density, pack-house standards, and retail partnerships
Dairy and livestock products	Strong domestic base	Breed improvement, traceability, and quality-linked pay
Organic and natural	High interest in global markets	Cluster-based organic certification and premium retail channels

APEDA and state agencies are working to deepen certification, brand presence, and last-mile trade infrastructure.

Sustainability and balance

Growth must protect the base. That means healthy soils, efficient water use, climate-smart seed choice, and cropping systems that keep nutrients in balance. Micro-irrigation, mulching, precise application of fertiliser, and rotations that include pulses help rebuild soil. The fisheries and aquaculture segment has also grown within the agricultural economy, lifting its share of value in recent years.

Empowering farmers: policy and institutions

Reform is most effective when it strengthens the farmer's hand.

- **Farmer-Producer Organisations** help households gain bargaining power and access services at scale.
- **Direct Benefit Transfers** route support to intended beneficiaries with less leakage.
- **Insurance and credit** smooth shocks and enable prudent risk-taking.
- **E-NAM and other market rails** widen access and improve price discovery.
- **Rural infrastructure,** such as roads, cold rooms, and warehouses, cuts waste and raises realised value.

These directions align with current national and state efforts and can be sequenced district by district.

A practical vision to 2035

With steady investment in irrigation, storage, extension, climate-smart seed, and market connectivity, agriculture and allied activities can expand value while keeping resource use in check. The aim is clear: resilient yields, higher farm-gate incomes, strong participation by women and youth, and a larger share of value addition in rural districts.

Headline indicators that anchor the vision

Indicator	Today	Direction of travel by 2035
Workers in agriculture and allied sectors	**-45.8%** of workers (2022-23)	More productive on-farm jobs; orderly movement to higher-value services in rural clusters
Share of GVA	**-18.3%** (2022-23)	Higher value per hectare through processing and quality upgrades
Foodgrain output	**330.5 MT** (record, 2022-23)	Stable growth with climate resilience and reduced loss
Horticulture output	**-352-355 MT** (2022-23)	Faster growth with cold-chain density and export readiness
Agri exports	**-USD 53.1 bn** (FY23)	Larger share of processed and premium categories
Agritech base	**-2,800 recognised startups** (Dec 2023)	Wider adoption of precision, traceability, and fintech tools

Agriculture is more than a sector. It is memory, skill, and shared purpose. When fields prosper, classrooms fill, small factories hum, and kitchens are secure. The task ahead is straightforward and worthy. Equip farmers with water where needed, advice when it matters, storage at the right point, and fair, open markets. Back science that respects the soil. Keep women and youth at the centre.

Combine this with India's human capital, and the country moves towards a future that is self-reliant, competitive, and environmentally sound. The fields of India do not only produce crops. They grow stability, confidence, and the quiet courage to feed a nation and the wider world.

Mineral Wealth: Powering Industry

India's path to industrial strength runs deep beneath her soil. From ancient crucible steel in Tamilakam to Kolar's storied seams of gold, geology has long served craft, trade, and state. In the modern economy, minerals feed power plants and cement kilns, shape rails and bridges, and enter every circuit from smartphones to satellites. When these resources are used wisely and with care for people and land, they build resilience at home and influence abroad.

Minerals touch nearly every sector: **coal for power**, **iron ore for steel**, **bauxite for aluminium**, **limestone for construction**, and **rare earths for electronics and clean energy**. India already sits near the top of global league tables for several of these, yet the space to rise higher remains. **Mining and quarrying contributed roughly 2.7% to GVA in recent official readings**, and policy aims to raise this share through faster exploration, transparent auctions, and value addition inside India.

India's Mineral Landscape and Global Standing

India reports **95+ minerals in the official basket** across fuel, metallic, and non-metallic groups, spread from the Himalaya to the Deccan and the coasts. Production in key streams, iron ore, limestone, bauxite, and coal, has set fresh records in recent years, signalling a broad base for industry.

At a Glance: Scale Indicators (latest official snapshots)

Indicator	Latest verified figure	Why it matters
Geological coal resources (to 1,200 m)	**378.21 billion tonnes (as on 01-Apr-2023)**	Long runway for domestic power and steel.
Coal production	**-998 million tonnes in FY 2023-24 (record)**	More secure power supply and lower import exposure.
Iron ore production	**-275-277 million tonnes in FY 2023-24 (record)**	Strong feedstock for steel growth.
Limestone production	**-450 million tonnes in FY 2023-24 (record)**	Supports cement and infrastructure.
Primary aluminium output (calendar 2023)	**-4.1-4.2 million tonnes; world #2**	Enables aviation, power, EVs.
Crude steel output (2023/24)	**-144 Mt; India is world #2**	Backbone metal for rails, roads, housing, and defence.
Rare earths in monazite	**-7.23 Mt REO within -13.15 Mt monazite**	Strategic input for magnets, electronics, wind, EVs.

Context notes: Ancient **wootz** (southern Indian crucible steel) powered a historic export craft; **Kolar**

Gold Fields produced for over a century before closure in 2001, leaving a deep technical legacy.

Key Mineral Resources and Their Potential

India's mineral belt runs across **Odisha, Chhattisgarh, Jharkhand, Karnataka, Rajasthan, and Andhra Pradesh**, among others. Reserves and resources vary by mineral; policy now pushes for more exploration, faster auctioning, and domestic processing to capture value within India.

Core minerals: what India holds and where it can go

Mineral	India's latest scale indicator	Global standing	Major uses	Practical potential
Coal	**Geological resources -378 Bt**; output -998 Mt FY24	Among the top producers	Power, sponge iron, cement	Cleaner power with higher efficiency units, gasification, and CCUS pilots to manage emissions.
Iron ore	Output -275–277 Mt FY24; large hematite/magnetite resources	Top-tier producer	Steel	Stable ore feed supports the push towards **300 Mt steel capacity by 2030-31**.
Bauxite / Aluminium	Bauxite resources -3.9 Bt (IBM); primary Al -4.1–4.2 Mt in 2023	**World #2** in primary aluminium	Aviation, power, EVs, packaging	Room to add value in rolled/ extruded products and low-carbon smelting.
Limestone	Output -450 Mt FY24	Large producer	Cement, construction	Supports rapid housing and transport build-out.
Rare earths (monazite)	**-7.23 Mt REO in -13.15 Mt monazite**	High global endowment	Electronics, magnets, wind, and defence	Beach-sand value chains and partnerships for separation, metals, and magnets.
Copper	Low share of world reserves; domestic ore is limited	Net importer of refined copper	Power grids, electronics, EVs	Smelter growth and overseas offtake tie-ups bridge the gap while new finds mature.
Gold	Legacy mines (KGF closed 2001); active belts in Karnataka & beyond	Small domestic output	Reserve asset, jewellery	New exploration and selective reopenings can curb import reliance at the margin.

Why this matters: a stronger minerals base lowers input risk for steel, cement, power, and electronics, and lifts India's position in supply chains where reliability is prized.

Coal and energy minerals: the power source

Coal still anchors the electricity supply. The **record -998 Mt output in FY24** helped build plant stocks and reduce thermal coal import exposure. The policy direction is clear: raise mining productivity, keep grids stable, and pair this with a faster build-out of non-fossil capacity. Cleaner pathways, **supercritical units, gasification, waste-heat recovery, and early CCUS pilots** can cut emissions intensity while renewables scale.

Iron and Steel: The Backbone of Industrialisation

India is **the world's second-largest crude steel producer**, with output around **144 Mt in 2023/24** and capacity nearing **-180–200 Mt**. Demand from housing, roads, rail, autos, and defence keeps rising. Securing ore quality, logistics, low-carbon energy, and scrap flows will help India hold price competitiveness and expand finished steel exports to regions in Africa and Southeast Asia.

Bauxite, aluminium, and the light-metal push

Aluminium supports aircraft, power gear, transport fleets, and renewable hardware. With **-4.1-4.2 Mt primary aluminium** in 2023, India stands at

world #2, and can climb the value chain in can-stock, EV components, and alloy products. Gains in energy efficiency and greener power inputs strengthen cost and carbon footprints together.

Rare Earths and Strategic Minerals

The twenty-first century leans on magnets and batteries the way the last century leaned on oil. India holds **-7.23 Mt of REO in monazite**, mainly along the eastern and southern coasts. Turning this endowment into separated oxides, metals, and magnet components needs technology partnerships and careful environmental management. Collaboration with trusted allies spreads risk and accelerates capability.

Gold and Precious Minerals: Wealth with Stability

Gold carries cultural weight and macro value. Domestic mining is modest today, yet belts in **Karnataka, Rajasthan, and Jharkhand** continue to see exploration. **Kolar Gold Fields**, once a mainstay, closed in 2001; fresh technology and selective projects can still add supply and skilled jobs in mining districts.

Sustainable and Responsible Mining

Growth must walk with stewardship. The path forward is straightforward: plan with communities, **reclaim mined areas**, recycle water, cut emissions at the site, and publish data that builds trust. When firms use renewable power on-site, track land and biodiversity outcomes, and invest in local health and education, the result is a licence to operate that lasts.

Responsible Mining: pillars and Field Actions

Pillar	Field action that works
Land & water	Concurrent reclamation, topsoil management, rainwater harvesting, and zero-liquid discharge, where feasible
Air & energy	Electrified haulage where viable, conveyor systems, renewable power PPAs, and real-time air monitoring
Safety & health	Global best-practice HIRA, dust control, occupational health checks, and community clinics
Community	Local hiring, skill centres, school support, grievance redressal, share of DMF funds to visible projects

Policy, Investment, and a Forward View

Reforms under the **National Mineral Policy 2019** and related rules aim to speed exploration and grant mining rights through transparent auctions, while building downstream value chains for steel, aluminium, cement, and advanced materials. Priorities include:

1. **More exploration spending** and modern surveys to convert resources into reserves.
2. **Private participation and FDI** in mining and processing, with strong safeguards.
3. **Domestic value chains** that keep refining and component-making inside India.
4. **Strategic stockpiles** for critical minerals.
5. **R&D** in low-impact extraction, beneficiation, and recycling.

Sector arcs to 2035 (Directional, Policy-linked)

Segment	Today (official snapshots)	Direction to 2035
Coal & power feed	**Resources -378 Bt; output -998 Mt FY24**	Higher efficiency, lower import reliance, and emission-intensity cuts via technology.
Metals (iron, steel, aluminium)	**Steel -144 Mt; aluminium -4.1-4.2 Mt**	Stronger downstream products, greener energy inputs, and logistics upgrades.
Critical minerals (REEs, copper, battery inputs)	**REE endowment -7.23 Mt REO; copper reserves limited**	Separation, metals, magnets in India; copper smelting capacity addition and overseas offtake ties.

Mineral wealth is more than ore. It is energy for families and factories, rails that connect markets, cement that shelters cities, and metals that carry the current of a digital age. When India explores with science, extracts with care, and processes at home, minerals turn into strength that is felt in jobs, exports, and national confidence.

If **agriculture feeds** and **human capital invents**, minerals provide the sturdy frame for industry to grow tall. The measure of success will not be tonnes alone; it will be whether mines lift districts, whether plants run cleaner, and whether India stands ready to supply the world with materials that are reliable, responsibly made, and proudly Indian.

Water and Energy: Lifelines of Growth

Water and energy carry the nation forward. They feed fields and factories, cool steel and lift data, light homes and move trains. India is fortunate in rivers, sunlight, and wind. The task is to use them wisely, protect them, and link them so that growth feels steady in every district and every season.

India receives close to **4,000 billion cubic metres (BCM)** of rainfall each year. River flows add up near **1,869 BCM**, yet only **around 1,120 BCM** can be used reliably because rain arrives in a short window and storage is limited. That reality explains why floods and droughts can visit different regions within the same year and why better storage, aquifer recharge, and recycling matter.

India is also **the world's third-largest energy consumer**, and electricity demand has risen quickly with new homes, appliances, and expanding industry. Investment has followed, with a strong tilt toward clean energy over the last five years.

The Power of Rivers and Water Systems

From the Ganga and Brahmaputra in the north to the Godavari, Krishna, and Kaveri in the south, rivers have built soils, carried trade, and driven turbines. Pressure has grown with fast urbanisation and intensive farming. Seasonal dependence on the monsoon creates swings, and pollution reduces usable supply in several basins. The answer is basin-level planning, modern storage, recharge of groundwater, and strong urban wastewater cycles that return treated water to farms and industry.

Major river regions: purpose and pressure

Region	Major rivers	Key benefits	Main challenges
North & Central	Ganga, Yamuna, Brahmaputra, Narmada	Irrigation, hydropower, navigation, drinking water	Pollution loads, sedimentation, over-abstraction
South	Godavari, Krishna, Kaveri, Periyar, Tungabhadra	Irrigation, cities, power	Seasonal flow variation, interstate tensions
West	Sabarmati, Mahi, Tapi	Urban supply, industry	Salinity ingress, over-extraction
East & North-East	Subarnarekha, Mahanadi, Barak	Flood control, delta agriculture, hydropower	Infrastructure gaps, erosion risk

Efficient management points in one direction: **river-basin authorities, wastewater reuse, micro-irrigation, reservoir modernisation, and aquifer recharge**. These steps convert the same drop into more value with less conflict.

India's Energy Landscape

India's energy system is changing shape. Coal still carries a large share of electricity, while oil fuels transport, yet non-fossil capacity has risen fast, and clean energy is now the bulk of power-sector investment. **Installed renewable energy, excluding large hydro, crossed 220 GW by March 2025**, with solar leading additions. **Non-fossil sources supplied roughly one-third of electricity in 2025**, marking a structural shift.

Installed capacity snapshot (latest official)

Segment	Capacity
Solar (grid-connected cumulative, MNRE)	**127.33 GW**
Wind (MNRE)	**-53 GW**
Renewable total excl. large hydro (MNRE)	**-220 GW**
Large hydro potential identified	**-145 GW**
Large hydro installed (≥25 MW, CEA)	**-50 GW**
Nuclear	**-7 GW**

Direction of travel: 500 GW of non-fossil capacity is the 2030 target. Multiple reports confirm that annual additions are rising, though transmission and storage must keep pace.

Solar Energy: Power from The Sun

India enjoys **300 to 330 clear days** each year across many regions, which is why solar scales quickly. The **National Institute of Solar Energy** assessed **748 GW** of potential on a modest share of wasteland. New assessments expand the view: recent studies point to **multi-terawatt potential** once rooftops, reservoirs, and other sites are included.

Installed solar crossed **127 GW** on MNRE's latest dashboard. A growing storage pipeline, green hydrogen pilots, and floating solar at reservoirs widen options for round-the-clock power and water-smart design.

Solar: potential, present, path

Item	Figure	Note
Ground-mounted solar potential (2014 baseline)	**-748 GW**	NISE, using 3% of wasteland
Updated deployable potential (new macro studies)	**>3,000 GWp**	Macro reassessments widen sites
Installed capacity	**127.33 GW**	MNRE dashboard
Manufacturing build-out	**Cell and module capacity expanding toward 2027**	Industry and MNRE updates

Solar is already cutting import bills, creating skilled work in installation and O&M, and lowering urban emissions as metros, airports, and EV chargers integrate rooftop and carport systems.

Wind Energy: The Invisible Giant

Onshore wind stretches across Tamil Nadu, Gujarat, Maharashtra, Karnataka, Rajasthan, and new belts inland. **Potential was earlier mapped at 302 GW at 100-metre hub height** and **-695 GW at 120 metres**, with taller towers opening more land. Installed capacity stands near **53 GW**, and offshore blocks off Gujarat and Tamil Nadu are moving through approvals. Blending wind with solar gives a natural complement across day and night.

Wind: potential and progress

Item	Figure	Source
Gross onshore potential at 100 m	**-302 GW**	NIWE
Gross onshore potential at 120 m	**-695 GW**	NIWE
Installed wind capacity	**-53 GW**	MNRE
Offshore indicative potential (Tamil Nadu + Gujarat coastlines)	**-70 GW**	NIWE and state briefs

Hydropower: the oldest renewable

Hydropower provides firm, flexible electricity and supports irrigation and flood moderation. **Potential near 145 GW** has been mapped for large hydro, with **around 50 GW installed**, plus small hydro beyond that. **Pumped-storage hydro** is now central for storing surplus solar and wind so power remains steady through the evening peak.

Integrating Water and Energy Systems

Water and energy rely on one another. Cooling demands shape power-plant choice, while pumping and treatment shape electricity use. The next gains come from integrated designs.

- **Hydro-solar hybrids** place floating solar on reservoirs to cut evaporation and use existing grid links.
- **Wastewater-to-energy** turns city sludge into biogas for local grids.
- **Desalination on renewables** serves coastal cities without raising emissions.

These designs build resilience against climate swings and reduce wasted resources.

Water–energy nexus: examples that scale

Solution	Water benefit	Energy benefit
Floating solar on reservoirs	Evaporation cut, shared transmission	Mid-day output without new land
Pumped-storage hydro	Stores monsoon inflows	Peak power and grid balancing
Wastewater biogas	Cleaner rivers, sludge treated	Firm gas for city power and heat
Solar irrigation with meters	Lower groundwater draw	Daytime agricultural load on solar

Energy security and self-reliance

India aims for **energy independence by 2047** and **net-zero by 2070**. The direction includes domestic exploration where needed, a rapid build-out of renewables and storage, and new fuels such as ethanol, compressed biogas, and green hydrogen for hard-to-abate sectors.

Security milestones to watch

Goal	Public signal	What it unlocks
Universal, reliable access	Saubhagya delivered connections to **-2.86 crore households**; the next phase is quality of supply	Equal opportunity for study, health, and small enterprise
Lower import dependence	Energy-independence 2047 initiative	Resilience against price shocks
Cleaner grids	Non-fossil share rising, nuclear expansion signalled	Stable, low-carbon growth path

Rural electrification and inclusive growth

Village electrification is near-universal, and household connections expanded at speed under **Saubhagya**, with states reporting **around 2.86 crore households** connected by March 2022. The next step is reliability: fewer outages, better voltage, and fair tariffs. Decentralised systems such as solar micro-grids, community biogas, and productive-use appliances lift incomes by powering irrigation, food processing, cold storage, clinics, and digital services.

Challenges and The Path Forward

- **Uneven water availability** across basins demands storage where it is scarce and flood moderation where it is abundant.
- **Pollution and leakage** waste scarce supply.

- **Grid losses** remain material; **AT&C losses fell to around 15.4% in FY23**, yet further decline is essential.
- **Finance and transmission** must scale with renewables and storage.

Priority fixes that pay back quickly

Issue	Action
Water stress in dry basins	Micro-irrigation, managed aquifer recharge, treated-water reuse
Urban and industrial pollution	Strict effluent enforcement, city-scale reuse mandates
Grid losses	Smart metering, feeder segregation, and high-voltage distribution systems
Renewable integration	Green corridors, storage tenders, flexible thermal operations

Water feeds the soil and cools the wire. Sunlight and wind feed the grid. When river basins are cared for, when storage is planned, when renewables grow with transmission and storage beside them, development holds steady. India's advantage is variety: snow-fed rivers and coastal deltas, bright skies and steady winds, a public that adapts fast when tools are clear and benefits are shared.

This is a future where energy reaches every home and workshop, where each drop is used more than once, where the bill is lower because the system wastes less, and where the air grows cleaner each year. The work is practical and within reach: measure well, build wisely, include communities, and keep science close to policy. Done that way, India leads in sustainability the same way it leads in scale.

Renewable potential and programme scale

Type	Technical potential	Current utilisation	2030-35 direction
Solar	**748 GW** baseline on wasteland; **>3,000 GWp** on expanded sites	**127.33 GW**	Storage-linked growth, rooftop and floating solar expansion
Wind (onshore)	**302 GW at 100 m; 695 GW at 120 m**	**-53 GW**	Repowering old sites; hybrid parks; offshore pilots
Hydro (large)	**-145 GW**	**-50 GW**	Pumped-storage for balancing; basin-level optimisation
Bioenergy	National programmes scaling	Gasifiers, CBG plants	Urban and agro-waste to energy at the city and cluster scale

Water stewardship: numbers that guide decisions

Metric	India value	What it implies
Average annual precipitation	**-4,000 BCM**	Storage and recharge convert a short wet season into a year-round supply
Natural runoff	**-1,869 BCM**	Basin-wise planning is essential
Utilizable water	**-1,120 BCM**	Reuse and efficiency raise the effective ceiling

Energy access and reliability

Indicator	Current status	Next step
Household connections under Saubhagya	**-2.86 crore households** connected	Improve reliability and voltage quality
AT&C losses	**-15.4% (FY23)**	Smart metering and feeder upgrades
Non-fossil electricity share	**-one-third in 2025**	Transmission corridors and storage scale-up

Tourism and Geography: India's Soft Power

Tourism is identity in motion. It carries stories from one heart to another, turns heritage into livelihood, and lets the world meet a country at its best. Few nations hold as much variety in one map as India does: ice fields and coral reefs, deserts and rainforests, shrine towns and high-tech cities. The land is generous, and the people are warmer still. That blend, place, and welcome make tourism a quiet engine of pride, income, and influence.

India's recovery since the pandemic has been strong. **Foreign Tourist Arrivals (FTAs) reached 9.52 million in 2023** (87% of 2019 and rising), while **domestic tourist visits crossed 2.51 billion** the same year. **Foreign exchange earnings from tourism touched US$28.08 billion in 2023**, and India accounted for **2.1% of worldwide tourism receipts**. These are not small steps; they are a base for the next climb.

India's geographic advantage

Variety is India's signature. Each region can host more than one kind of travel culture, nature, wellness, learning, adventure, often in the same journey.

Regions, features, and travel strengths

Region	Natural and cultural features	Travel strengths	Illustrative magnets
North	Himalaya, glaciers, valleys, shrine towns	Adventure, mountaineering, spiritual circuits	Kashmir, Himachal, Uttarakhand
South	Coasts, backwaters, temple architecture, spice hills	Cultural routes, wellness, beaches, houseboats	Kerala, Tamil Nadu, Karnataka
West	That desert, forts, stepwells, and long coastline	Heritage trails, desert safaris, leisure beaches	Rajasthan, Goa, Gujarat
East & North-East	Hills, tea gardens, forests, river islands	Eco and community tourism, heritage	Odisha, Sikkim, Assam
Central	Tiger reserves, caves, plateaus	Wildlife, eco-parks, caving	Madhya Pradesh, Chhattisgarh

UNESCO recognition keeps growing; India now has **44 World Heritage Sites**, reflecting both cultural wealth and natural beauty. Improved access underpins this arc: **operational airports rose to 157 in 2024**, with a long-term plan to expand further by 2047.

Tourism as a driver of economic growth

Travel creates work where people live, guides, artisans, homestays, transport, food, and festivals. The **WTTC projects Travel & Tourism at INR 21.15 trillion in 2024** (roughly one in eleven jobs), with spending growth in both international and domestic segments. The **India Tourism Data Compendium 2024** confirms a broad rebound in arrivals, receipts, and visits through 2023.

Scale markers that matter (latest official)

Indicator	2019	2023	Note
Foreign Tourist Arrivals (million)	**10.93**	**9.52**	Recovery to 87% of 2019; trend positive.
Foreign Exchange Earnings (US$ bn)	–	**28.08**	Provisional 2023 estimate.
Domestic tourist visits (million)	–	**2,509.63**	Up -45% over 2022.
India's share of world tourism receipts	–	**-2.1%**	UNWTO referenced in Compendium.

The implication is clear: with steady marketing, better connectivity, and strong service standards, tourism can raise incomes in every state.

Types of tourism and their potential

India's portfolio spans culture, wellness, religious travel, wildlife and adventure, higher education, meetings, medical care, and film trails. Rather than guess counts by segment, anchor the plan on verified totals and targeted growth.

Portfolio view: what to scale and how

Segment	Current footing	What to scale by 2035
Cultural & heritage	**44 UNESCO sites**; strong city circuits	City heritage upgrades, night-time economies, craft markets, and multilingual guiding.
Religious & spiritual	High domestic footfall to shrine towns; steady FTA share	Pilgrim amenities, green mobility, crowd management, and water-waste treatment.
Health & wellness	Ayurveda, yoga, and naturopathy alongside modern care	Clinic accreditation, insurance tie-ups, wellness routes (Kerala-Rishikesh hubs).
Eco & adventure	National parks and Himalayan routes; community homestays	Carrying-capacity rules, certified operators, safety infrastructure, and green stays.
Educational & knowledge	English-medium, competitive fees, research clusters	"Study in India," dual-degree tracks, internships with local industry.
MICE & film	New convention spaces, film facilitation	Event pipelines, single-window clearances, destination branding.

If India sustains its present momentum and expands air, rail, and digital rails, a **top-five global tourism economy** by the mid-2030s is within reach; domestic demand and inbound long-haul both contribute.

Health and wellness tourism: the healing advantage

India's blend of clinical skill and traditional systems is distinctive. **Medical arrivals climbed to 4.75 lakh in 2022 and 5.04 lakh (Jan-Oct) in 2023,** per the Bureau of Immigration. Hospitals with **NABH** and **ISQua-recognised** quality systems anchor trust, while yoga and Ayurveda add prevention and recovery. Wellness resorts, meditation retreats, and post-procedure recovery stays complement city hospitals.

How to accelerate: package pricing transparency, recovery-friendly visas for attendants, and international insurance panels. For wellness, certification, and outcome tracking, build credibility.

Cultural heritage: the soul at work

Heritage is living: language, music, cuisine, textiles, and festivals. When visitors buy handloom directly from a weaver or listen to a morning raga by the river, culture becomes income and dignity. Digital platforms now connect craft clusters with global buyers; curated night walks, museum hours, and riverfront performances keep spending within local communities. **The Taj Mahal remained the top ASI ticketed site in 2023**, showing how icons can anchor wider circuits.

Eco and adventure tourism: sustainability with thrill

National parks such as Corbett, Kaziranga, and Ranthambore continue to draw both domestic and foreign visitors. The Himalaya offers trekking and skiing routes that scale safely when carrying-capacity plans, certified guides, and waste rules are enforced. States like **Sikkim** and **Kerala** demonstrate how community-led tourism protects forests while raising incomes. The path is simple: certify operators, grow **eco-lodges**, push low-emission transport, and create **carbon-neutral zones** where feasible.

Education and knowledge tourism

Universities, research institutes, and skill academies attract learners from Asia, Africa, and beyond. The **Study in India** programme positions the country as a value-rich, English-medium hub with cultural immersion. Short schools, joint degrees, and industry internships turn study into experience and a long-term partnership.

Infrastructure and connectivity

Access makes or breaks a destination. India's aviation build-out has been decisive: **operational airports doubled to 157 by 2024**, while new highways, metros, and semi-high-speed rail improve the last mile. Digital rails matter too: **UPI** gives visitors seamless payments across cities and small towns.

Enablers that lift every destination

Enabler	Status	What to add next
Airports and routes	**157 operational airports (2024)**	More tier-2/3 connectivity; night landing; regional MRO hubs.
Rail and road	National corridors, expressways, and metro growth	Scenic trains, smart bus stations, EV tourist fleets.
Digital payments	Near-universal UPI acceptance	Tourist wallets, multilingual support, tax-refund pilots.

Soft image and global influence

Soft power grows when experience matches promise. Yoga, films, food, festivals, and scholarship keep India present in global minds. **International Day of Yoga**, led worldwide each June, is a simple, universal invitation that begins with wellbeing and ends in friendship.

Challenges and The Path Forward

- **Gaps in sanitation and connectivity** at remote sites
- **Perception issues** that require consistent global marketing with real service upgrades
- **Ecological stress** from crowding at peak times
- **Skill depth** in guiding, languages, safety, and digital operations

Policy tools already in motion, National Tourism Policy consultations, destination management plans, and **Dekho Apna Desh** can close these gaps when states, industry, and communities plan together.

Practical fixes with quick payback

Issue	Field fix
Overcrowding at icons	Timed entries, night hours, dispersal to secondary sites
Waste and pollution	City-level reuse of treated water; strict solid-waste contracts
Service quality	State skill missions for guides, drivers, homestays; multilingual apps
Safety and compliance	Certified adventure operators; emergency cover on key trails

Vision 2035: a global tourism powerhouse

By the mid-2030s, India can be among the world's top destinations on both volume and value. The route is clear: double inbound in measured steps, keep domestic travel thriving, and build sustainability into every itinerary. Health, heritage, nature, learning, and meetings each carry part of the load; together they create reliable jobs and a larger soft footprint.

Headline targets to organise the effort (directional)

Pillar	2023 baseline	2035 direction
FTAs	**9.52 million**	High-teens to low-twenties (million) with deeper long-haul share
Foreign exchange earnings	**US$28.08 bn**	Higher value per visitor through longer stays and cultural spending

(Continued..)

Domestic visits	**2.51 billion**	Wider spread to tier-2/3 circuits; seasonal balance
Medical and wellness	**5.04 lakh arrivals (Jan-Oct 2023)**	Higher accreditation coverage; insurance-linked flows

India's wealth is more than mines and machines. It lives in hospitality, craft, music, cuisines, and the welcome at the doorstep. Tourism turns this wealth into livelihoods and friendships. When airports and roads bring people in, when cities are clean and safe, when parks are protected and guides are trained, visitors carry home a story that lifts the country's image long after the trip ends.

The message is steady and bright: the map is varied, the culture is deep, and the doors are open. With care for nature and care for people, India can grow tourism that feels proud, fair, and future-proof, one journey at a time.

Tourism and Geography: India's Soft Power

Tourism is identity moving across borders, a meeting of places and people that turns memory into livelihood and pride into work. India holds a rare variety within one map, where snow peaks and coral beds share the same passport as shrine towns, tea slopes, dune seas, backwaters, and quicksilver cities. Visitors come for scenery and history, yet they carry home something deeper, since the welcome matters as much as the view, and the conversation often lingers longer than the monument.

India's strength here is simple to state and rich to build on. Travel brings income to homes that might stand far from factories, it gives crafts a paying audience, it fills seasons with work for guides, drivers, cooks, and artists, and it keeps culture present rather than preserved behind glass.

India's geographic advantage

Few countries can host so many kinds of journeys without leaving their borders. The north opens valleys and glaciers, the west stretches into desert and fort country, the south offers coasts, temples, and waters that wind through palm and spice, the east and the North-East bring tea gardens and forests, while the centre folds in jungles and caves. This range makes room for cultural routes, wellness retreats, wildlife holidays, city breaks, mountain treks, pilgrim circuits, and field schools for students. India's position between regions of Asia and across sea lanes helps further, since flights keep growing and roads and rail knit the long distances into trips that feel possible within one itinerary.

Regions, features, and travel strengths

Region	Natural and cultural features	Travel strengths	Illustrative magnets
North	Himalaya, glaciers, valleys, shrine towns	Adventure, mountaineering, spiritual circuits	Kashmir, Himachal, Uttarakhand
South	Coasts, backwaters, temple architecture, spice hills	Cultural routes, wellness, beaches, houseboats	Kerala, Tamil Nadu, Karnataka

(Continued..)

West	Thar desert, forts, stepwells, and long coastline	Heritage trails, desert safaris, leisure beaches	Rajasthan, Goa, Gujarat
East & North-East	Hills, tea gardens, forests, river islands	Eco and community tourism, heritage	Odisha, Sikkim, Assam
Central	Tiger reserves, caves, plateaus	Wildlife, eco-parks, caving	Madhya Pradesh, Chhattisgarh

UNESCO recognition keeps growing. India now has **44 World Heritage Sites**, reflecting both cultural wealth and natural beauty. Improved access underpins this arc: **operational airports rose to 157 in 2024**, with a long-term plan to expand further by 2047.

Tourism as a driver of economic growth

Travel money reaches many hands. A guesthouse buys vegetables from a nearby farm, an artisan sees fresh demand for work that a family learned from elders, a young graduate trains as a guide and then studies a second language to widen options. Earnings in cities spread to surrounding districts when supply chains are local, and every season adds to confidence when service improves and access grows.

Scale markers that matter (latest official)

Indicator	2019	2023	Note
Foreign Tourist Arrivals (million)	**10.93**	**9.52**	Recovery to 87% of 2019; trend positive.
Foreign Exchange Earnings (US$ bn)	–	**28.08**	Provisional 2023 estimate.
Domestic tourist visits (million)	–	**2,509.63**	Up -45% over 2022.
India's share of world tourism receipts	–	**-2.1%**	UNWTO referenced in Compendium.

The implication is clear: with steady marketing, better connectivity, and strong service standards, tourism can raise incomes in every state.

Types of tourism and their potential

India's portfolio is broad and resilient. Cultural travel will always draw those who want to see great buildings and living art, wellness grows with every person who seeks recovery or balance, religious travel fills trains and buses year-round, wildlife and adventure bring a different pace to hills and forests, while education and knowledge travel place students inside labs, studios, and field projects. The plan is to strengthen each stream without crowding any place beyond its capacity.

Portfolio view: what to scale and how

Segment	Current footing	What to scale by 2035
Cultural & heritage	**44 UNESCO sites**; strong city circuits	City heritage upgrades, night-time economies, craft markets, and multilingual guiding.
Religious & spiritual	High domestic footfall to shrine towns; steady FTA share	Pilgrim amenities, green mobility, crowd management, and water-waste treatment.
Health & wellness	Ayurveda, yoga, and naturopathy alongside modern care	Clinic accreditation, insurance tie-ups, wellness routes (Kerala–Rishikesh hubs).
Eco & adventure	National parks and Himalayan routes; community homestays	Carrying-capacity rules, certified operators, safety infrastructure, and green stays.
Educational & knowledge	English-medium, competitive fees, research clusters	"Study in India," dual-degree tracks, internships with local industry.
MICE & film	New convention spaces, film facilitation	Event pipelines, single-window clearances, destination branding.

If India sustains its present momentum and expands air, rail, and digital rails, a **top-five global tourism economy** by the mid-2030s is within reach; domestic demand and inbound long-haul both contribute.

Health and wellness tourism: the healing advantage

Care has two strands in India that work best together. Hospitals deliver complex procedures at high standards with costs that many families abroad find within reach, and traditional systems such as Ayurveda and Yoga offer prevention, recovery, and calm, which modern life often fails to provide. When a patient or a traveller can find clarity on pricing, quality accreditation, and post-care support, trust grows quickly, and that trust brings companions and referrals. Destinations like Rishikesh and Kerala already lead with retreats and clinics that value both science and serenity, and they show how wellness can create steady local work without heavy strain on land or water.

Cultural heritage: the soul at work

Heritage lives when people practise it. A weaver who sells directly to a visitor earns fairly and keeps a craft alive for another season, a classical concert by a river changes how a traveller hears a city, a museum that stays open into the evening lengthens stay and spending without any extra concrete. Icons such as the Taj Mahal hold world attention, yet nearby towns and lesser-known sites turn a single stop into a circuit that spreads income more evenly. Digital platforms now carry craft to global buyers, and those buyers often become visitors, closing a loop between culture online and journeys on the ground.

Eco and adventure tourism: sustainability with thrill

Forests, high meadows, and river islands ask for care before crowds. The lesson is clear wherever it has been tried well: set carrying capacities, certify operators, train guides, plan rescue cover, handle waste with discipline, and make the local community a partner who shares both responsibility and reward. When this happens, wildlife remains healthy, trails stay open, and young people find work that keeps them in the places they love. States that place community at the centre and plan for seasons rather than weekends see visitor satisfaction rise while pressure on nature falls.

Education and knowledge tourism

Students who arrive for degrees, short-term schools, or internships become long-term friends of the country. English-medium teaching helps, costs are often reasonable, and campus life opens doors to cultural learning that stays with a person far beyond exams. Stronger links between universities and industry create projects that feel real, and cultural immersion turns alumni into repeat visitors who bring families and colleagues later in life. The **Study in India** initiative can grow faster when credits transfer smoothly and internships slot into term breaks without friction.

Infrastructure and connectivity

Access makes a place visible. More airports bring more routes, rail projects shorten journeys between key cities, and smooth highways pull smaller towns onto travel maps that once focused only on metro circuits. Digital rails matter too. UPI lets a traveller pay a tea stall and a museum with the same tap, which lowers hassle and builds trust.

Enablers that lift every destination

Enabler	Status	What to add next
Airports and routes	**157 operational airports (2024)**	More tier-2/3 connectivity; night landing; regional MRO hubs.
Rail and road	National corridors, expressways, and metro growth	Scenic trains, smart bus stations, EV tourist fleets.
Digital payments	Near-universal UPI acceptance	Tourist wallets, multilingual support, tax-refund pilots.

The power of soft image and global influence

Soft power grows when visitors feel cared for and carry that story home. Yoga gatherings in public parks, film festivals that showcase local and regional cinema, food trails that honour both street stalls and new kitchens, and cultural institutes that host talks and workshops create a daily presence that advertising cannot buy. Tourism becomes a form of friendship when the welcome feels real and the exchange is two-way.

Challenges and the path forward

Some gaps remain, and they are solvable. Remote sites need clean toilets, safe water, clear paths, and reliable transport. Crowd pressure at famous places needs timed entries that protect both monument and mood. Skills must deepen in languages, guiding, safety, and digital systems for bookings and reviews. Marketing should match reality on the ground so that promise and delivery stay aligned.

Practical fixes with quick payback

Issue	Field fix
Overcrowding at icons	Timed entries, night hours, dispersal to secondary sites
Waste and pollution	City-level reuse of treated water; strict solid-waste contracts
Service quality	State skill missions for guides, drivers, homestays; multilingual apps
Safety and compliance	Certified adventure operators; emergency cover on key trails

Vision 2035: India as a global tourism powerhouse

The direction is steady. Keep foreign arrivals rising in careful steps, keep domestic travel affordable and connected, spread benefits to tier-2 and tier-3 cities and rural circuits, and place sustainability at the centre so that the same river, the same trail, and the same festival can welcome more people each year without losing what makes it special.

Headline targets to organise the effort (directional)

Pillar	2023 baseline	2035 direction
FTAs	**9.52 million**	High-teens to low-twenties (million) with deeper long-haul share
Foreign exchange earnings	**US$28.08 bn**	Higher value per visitor through longer stays and cultural spending
Domestic visits	**2.51 billion**	Wider spread to tier-2/3 circuits; seasonal balance
Medical and wellness	**5.04 lakh arrivals (Jan-Oct 2023)**	Higher accreditation coverage; insurance-linked flows

India's wealth here is human and natural at once. A smile at a doorway, a story told well, a craft learned over years, a forest that stays alive because its guardians can earn with dignity, a temple town that welcomes pilgrims with clean streets and fair prices, a clinic that heals and a retreat that restores. Tourism gathers all of this into a movement that strengthens families and raises the country's standing without strain or noise. With care for sites and care for people, India can grow a travel economy that feels proud, fair, and future-ready, turning visits into friendships and journeys into shared progress.

Intellectual and Knowledge Capital: The Mind of India

Fields and factories build output; minds set direction. The asset that lasts is the habit of clear thought, patient inquiry, and useful invention. India carries an old discipline of learning and a young surge of creators; together, they form a strong base for this century.

The thread runs from early mathematics and medicine to satellites and software. It is a single stream where earlier insight meets new tools and turns into work that serves people.

A legacy that keeps working

Zero, place value, early algebraic methods, careful star charts, and surgical guidance were built for daily use rather than display. Scholars such as Aryabhata and Bhaskaracharya measured celestial movement with care and accuracy. Ayurveda and the Sushruta tradition paired observation with a method for the care of body and mind. Debates across schools trained generations to listen, test, and reason. The line from those classrooms to today's labs stays unbroken.

Modern systems that scale

Independent India chose science and technology for the public good. ISRO, CSIR, IISc, and the IIT system widened its capability one milestone at a time. In 2023, Chandrayaan-3 reached the lunar south pole region and proved what focused teams can do with frugal engineering. In 2024, Aditya-L1 settled into its halo orbit to study the Sun and opened fresh paths for space science. The software wave since the 1990s matured into platforms and digital public infrastructure for identity, payments, and records; adoption at scale brought lower costs and wider access. With internet use moving toward nine hundred million people, reach and learning expand season by season.

Where India stands among peers

India blends scale, affordability, and an ethos of building for many. Global rankings place the country high within its income group while leaving room to climb further.

Comparative knowledge strengths at a glance

Country	Knowledge capital strengths	Innovation drivers	Challenges
India	Mathematics to space science; fast-growing digital rails	Young talent; frugal invention; public platforms	Skills mismatch; uneven R&D spend
USA	Advanced research; strong patenting	Venture capital; deep university-industry links	High costs; ageing research cohort
Germany	Engineering depth; applied science	Dual education; precision manufacturing	Slower pivots in some digital areas
China	Scale in applied tech and manufacturing research	Mission-style programmes; rapid rollout	IP quality concerns; creativity limits

India's distinctive edge lies in mixing an old culture of learning with modern problem-solving for large populations.

Education and research engines

Scale is clear and quality is rising. The system now spans more than a thousand universities and tens of thousands of colleges; enrolment has grown sharply; capacity in medicine, engineering, and pure science has expanded. Alumni run global teams in technology and design, a signal that the training travels well.

R&D intensity needs a lift. National spending remains under one per cent of GDP in the standard series; moving toward one-and-a-half per cent would raise output, partnerships, and research careers.

Scale signals in education and research

Indicator	India
Universities (latest official count)	1,213
Higher-education institutions	58,643
Students in higher education	43.3 million
R&D spend (% of GDP, latest series)	< 1%

Raising faculty strength, funding core labs, and simplifying grants would accelerate progress; deeper links between campuses and firms would turn more theses into products and services.

Research, innovation, and startups

The venture base is now among the world's largest. Recognised startups passed 1.59 lakh, with strong participation by women directors. Activity spans fintech, healthtech, edtech, agritech, clean energy, and software products. Support programmes under Startup India and Digital India have supplied recognition, mentoring, market rails, and tax relief.

Momentum in the venture economy

Signal	Latest marker
DPIIT-recognised startups	1,59,157
Recognised startups with at least one woman director	73,151
Policy tailwinds	Startup India; Digital India; targeted 80-IAC relief

With steady capital, research tie-ins, and export access, the startup engine can add jobs across skills while solving Indian use-cases at scale.

Digital public goods and open rails

Aadhaar, UPI, DigiLocker, and allied stacks have lowered transaction costs and widened access for households and small firms. The same rails now support schools, clinics, welfare delivery, and local bodies. Partner countries study and adapt these systems, which extends India's intellectual influence into standards and shared protocols.

The next frontier

Priority fields stand out: artificial intelligence and data science with safety and inclusion at the core; biotechnology and life sciences with strong clinical evidence; space technology with growing commercial capacity; energy storage and green hydrogen that join science with manufacturing; and strategic technologies that reduce external risk. Shared roadmaps across labs, firms, and universities will keep momentum steady.

Ideas need protection and pathways.

Patents, designs, and copyrights help creators carry value across time and markets. India's filings and grants have risen; the debate now focuses on exam capacity, quality of claims, and stronger routes from filing to licensed products. University IP cells, standard-essential work, and fair licensing can shift focus from counting forms to building outcomes.

IP pulse, recent years

Indicator	**India**
Patent applications (FY 2023-24)	92,168
Patents granted (FY 2023-24)	1,03,057
Note	Examiner strength and process quality under active review

Joining heritage with frontier science

Traditional knowledge provides hypotheses; modern labs test and refine them. Ayurveda and Yoga sit beside biomedicine in trials and longitudinal studies. Number theory and combinatorics from classical texts inspire current algorithmic work. Ecological guidance from earlier treatises aligns with regenerative farming and water stewardship. The goal is a synthesis that meets scientific standards and helps people.

Frictions to face, choices to make

Brain drain follows thin lab budgets and limited equipment; steady investment and greater autonomy can reverse that flow. Curricula that reward projects and problem-solving raise employability. Policy should favour open science where possible and strong privacy where required. Communication that shares research in plain words builds public trust.

Vision 2040: a clear horizon

A practical horizon includes higher R&D spend toward two per cent of GDP; one hundred new centres of excellence in AI, biotech, space, and sustainability; global partnerships that produce shared labs, shared IP, and shared training; rewards for patent quality and commercialisation; and student pipelines that bring learners from every region into Indian labs and studios. On this path, knowledge adds growth, resilience, and dignity, with gains visible in cleaner energy, better medicines, safer transport, and accessible tools for work and learning.

Closing note

The mind of India is a workshop, not a showroom. From zero to lunar letters, from sutras to silicon, the thread holds steady: learn with care, build with purpose, and use knowledge to widen the chance for everyone. Feed curiosity, fund ideas, protect creation, and keep science close to everyday life. That is how a country moves from service to leadership and turns learning into a kinder world.

Scale signals that frame the decade

Domain	India now	Near-term direction
Internet users	Moving toward 900+ million	Wider rural reach; richer services on open rails
Global innovation standing	High within the income peer group	Rise with stronger R&D and campus-industry bridges
Space science	Chandrayaan-3 south-pole success; Aditya-L1 in halo orbit	Human spaceflight preparation; deeper science missions; new commercial lift
Startup base	1.59 lakh recognised ventures	More research spin-outs; healthy exits; export growth

Knowledge sectors and potential impact

Field	Current global share (%)	2035 target (%)	Potential GDP contribution (USD trillion)
IT & digital innovation	15	25	1.0
Research & higher education	3	10	0.7
Startups & entrepreneurship	6	12	0.8
Health & biotech research	4	9	0.5
Space & strategic technology	2	5	0.4

Knowledge ecosystem comparison

Item	India	USA	China	Germany
Internet users (million)	900	310	1,000	80
R&D spending (% of GDP)	0.9	2.8	2.2	3.1
Recognised startups	120,000+	600,000+	150,000+	60,000+
Annual graduates in STEM (million)	3.5	0.8	4.0	0.4
AI research output (rank)	5th	1st	2nd	4th

Startup sectors and 2035 outlook

Sector	Current startups (approx.)	Funding received (USD billion)	Potential GDP contribution by 2035 (USD billion)
Fintech	10,000	12	250
Healthtech	5,000	8	200
Edtech	3,000	5	150
Agritech	2,000	3	100
Renewable & clean tech	1,500	7	150
Total	**-21,500**	**-35**	**-850**

Education and Research Institutes: Foundations of Future Growth

A country rises on the strength of its classrooms as much as its factories. Schools and universities shape character, feed curiosity, and train hands and minds to solve real problems with grace. In India, learning carries the weight of tradition and the brightness of new ambition; the path runs from the gurukul to institutes that now send graduates to lead labs, companies, and clinics across the world. As the global economy leans on ideas and skill, India's education and research system stands as both an inheritance and engine, a living bridge between memory and invention.

A good system does more than teach letters and numbers. It builds judgement, cultivates compassion, and gives young people the confidence to learn through life. India's work now is to align reach with quality and to match scale with research depth, so that every student can find purpose in a century shaped by technology, design, and steady reinvention.

India's education ecosystem: a global giant in scale

India runs one of the largest education networks on Earth. The sweep is national, the intake immense, and the momentum unmistakable.

Scale and access

Level	Institutions (Approx.)	Enrolment (Million)	Gross Enrolment Ratio (GER)
Primary (Classes 1-5)	1.1 million	120	98%
Secondary (Classes 6-12)	0.4 million	90	80%
Higher Education	1,000+ universities & 40,000 colleges	38	28%

Access has widened across decades; the focus now turns to teaching quality, employability, research culture, and strong governance. The **National Education Policy 2020** sets direction for a multidisciplinary model rooted in Indian languages and values, with flexible pathways, skill integration, and clear standards for learning outcomes.

Ancient heritage of learning

Centres such as Nalanda, Takshashila, and Vikramshila welcomed scholars from far and near. Study covered grammar and logic, medicine and astronomy, statecraft and ethics; the goal was wisdom in practice. Reviving that spirit today means blending moral formation with science and technology, so graduates leave campus ready to serve society with creativity, rigour, and care.

Modern higher education and research institutions

After independence, India invested in scientific and technical pillars that endure. The IITs, IIMs, AIIMS, IISc, IISERs, and NITs created strong lanes for engineering, management, medicine, and fundamental science. Alumni now head global teams and shape policy, product, and research in many capitals.

India's contemporary pillars of learning

Type of institution	Examples	Focus area	Global recognition
Technical	IITs, NITs	Engineering; innovation; technology translation	Consistently ranked among the top groups in technology fields
Management	IIMs	Business; leadership; public policy	Frequent presence in global management listings
Science & research	IISc, IISERs	Advanced research; doctoral training	Strong reputations for scientific output

Medical	AIIMS, JIPMER	Medicine; public health; clinical research	High trust in care quality and training
Agriculture & environment	ICAR, FRI	Food security, climate science, and forestry	Leadership in applied research networks

Excellence concentrates in select clusters; the task ahead is to widen quality across regions through academic autonomy, fair funding, faculty development, and reliable infrastructure.

Comparative global position

India produces graduates at a great scale, yet research density and patenting per capita trail richer systems. The remedy lies in research-led teaching, experiential learning, and partnerships that move ideas from lab to field.

A quick comparison of output and emphasis

Country	Number of top institutions	Annual research papers	Employment potential	Focus area
India	50+	400,000+	High untapped potential	STEM; IT; management
USA	300+	1,500,000+	High innovation output	Advanced research; global patents
UK	80+	300,000+	Concentrated excellence	Sciences; humanities
China	100+	1,000,000+	Government-driven innovation	Applied technologies

Scale gives room to move; the next step is intensity of discovery and collaboration that produces visible impact.

Research and development: the missing link

National R&D spending remains below one per cent of GDP, which holds back breakthroughs. Strengthening research capacity will shift India from consumer to creator at speed. Promising moves include the **National Research Foundation** for interdisciplinary grants, the **Atal Innovation Mission** to inspire young builders, and deeper industry–academia projects that carry ideas to market.

With steady, well-governed funding and shared facilities, research output can climb sharply by 2035 in biotechnology, AI, materials, and energy storage, with thousands of quality patents and open-data publications each year.

Linking education to industry and employment

Employers seek practice-ready talent; new graduates often need bridges between the classroom and workplace. Four levers close the gap: vocational modules built into degrees; apprenticeships designed with firms; career guidance that spans school to first job; and state-level skill hubs specialising in local industry. If executed with care, these steps can turn the demographic dividend into higher productivity and higher household income over two decades.

Internationalisation of education

India attracts learners from Africa, the Middle East, and Southeast Asia through English-medium programmes, recognised qualifications, and competitive fees. **Studying in India** and **GIAN** bring visiting faculty, joint degrees, and shared research.

International education targets

Metric	Current (2025)	2035 target
Foreign students enrolled	75,000	300,000
Annual education export revenue	USD 10 billion	USD 50–70 billion
Global academic partnerships	250+	1,000+
Joint research centres	120	400

Education exports generate income and also strengthen India's cultural presence; alumni carry favourable stories for life.

Digital education and future learning models

The pandemic accelerated platforms and blended teaching. **SWAYAM** and **DIKSHA** opened courses to millions; private edtech added scale; low-cost data and digital public rails made access easier for families. The next leap joins classroom mentorship with AI tutors, AR or VR simulations for labs, and personalised pathways that keep learners engaged. By 2035, India can host the largest online learning market anywhere, serving both domestic and overseas students.

Teacher development and educational quality

Teachers anchor every reform. Continuous professional development, mentoring networks, and practical classroom tools raise learning in a way no policy can match. The **National Mission for Mentoring** under NEP 2020 focuses on this spine. Transparent evaluation that supports improvement, and partnerships with high-performing systems in Finland or Singapore, help adapt proven methods to Indian classrooms. When teachers thrive, communities feel it.

Challenges and reforms ahead

Five hurdles remain visible:

1. **Funding constraints**; public spending sits near three per cent of GDP, while policy points higher.
2. **Urban-rural gaps** in facilities and trained staff.

3. **Examination pressure** that favours recall over reasoning.
4. **Fragmented research** with weak bridges between institutes, government, and firms.
5. **Regulatory complexity** that slows fresh programmes and cross-campus collaboration.

NEP 2020 addresses structure: flexible curricula, credit mobility, multidisciplinary universities, digital inclusion, and assessment that values application and creativity.

Vision 2040: education as national power

By 2040, India can build a learning ecosystem that welcomes every child, lifts research to two per cent of GDP, and places one hundred universities among the world's top two hundred. Skill training belongs in all degree programmes; international exchanges and global campuses will bring scholars in and send scholars out. Education then becomes the nation's most generous export: knowledge, values, and invention that help solve shared problems in technology, sustainability, and public health.

Education renews a civilisation one cohort at a time. In India, it is memory and mission together. From ancient halls where debate prized truth, to digital classrooms where a village child can master code or design, the same flame moves forward. Invest wisely, honour teachers, open doors for research, and tie learning to dignity and work; the result is a country confident in mind and generous in spirit, a light that helps others find their way.

Horizon markers for access and excellence

Indicator	2025 (Current)	2035 Target	2040 Vision
Gross Enrolment Ratio: Higher Education	28%	50%	70%
R&D spending (% of GDP)	0.9%	1.5%	2.0%
Universities ranked in the Top 500	10	50	100
Foreign students	75,000	300,000	500,000
Education export revenue (USD billion)	10	50	100

Employment and GDP impact by segment

Education segment	Employment created (Million)	Contribution to GDP (USD billion)
Schools and teacher training	10	250
Higher education	8	400
Vocational and skill training	12	500
Digital education and edtech	6	300
Research and innovation	3	350
Total	**39**	**1,800+**

Creative and Entertainment Industry: The Cultural Wealth of India

Culture is the heartbeat that steadies a people, and creativity is the voice that carries that beat into daily life. India has lived with art for millennia, and that habit shows in every corner of the map: a poem recited in a small courtyard, hands folding silk on a loom, a raga rising at dawn, a mural brightening a quiet lane, a film that moves crowds to laughter and thought. The creative and entertainment industry is more than an economic sector; it is a working mirror of India's spirit, turning memory into livelihood and skill into pride.

India's cultural DNA: a civilisation of expression

From the Vedas and the Natya Shastra to the Ramayana and the Mahabharata, India's texts teach performance, story, beauty and ethics in the same breath, which is why art here feels woven into ordinary life. The line runs from Bhimbetka's caves to studios and stages today, with each region adding its own colour: Kathak in the north, Bharatanatyam in the south, Manipuri in the east, folk forms across the desert belt, papier-mâché in Kashmir, Kanchipuram silk in Tamil Nadu. This spread of practice is identity and economy together, since it carries both meaning and work to those who keep the forms alive.

The modern creative economy: scale and potential

India's creative system spans cinema, streaming, television, radio, print, music, theatre, crafts, design, gaming and the fast-growing world of digital creators. It supports millions directly, and many more through tourism, retail and technology. The base is broad, the talent is young, and new platforms shorten the distance between a maker and an audience.

Overview of India's creative economy

Sub-sector	Annual revenue (USD billion)	Employment (million)	Growth rate (%)
Film and television	20	3.5	10–12
Music industry	2	0.4	15
Digital media and OTT	5	0.6	25
Art, crafts and design	3	2.0	8
Publishing and literature	2	0.3	6
Total	**32**	**6.8**	**12.5 (avg)**

With steady investment, skill development and global distribution, the sector can rise toward 60 billion dollars by 2035 and pass ten million jobs, as language diversity and low entry barriers bring new voices to the fore.

Indian cinema: the world's largest storytelling industry

More than two thousand films appear each year across twenty-plus languages; volume is high, yet the real strength lies in range and audience connection. Mumbai's Hindi cinema remains a magnet, while regional film industries in Telugu, Tamil and Malayalam have built strong identities and loyal global audiences. Works such as *RRR*, *Baahubali*, *Dangal* and *Lagaan* showed how craft, scale and rooted themes can travel across borders. Three forces power the climb: streaming platforms that carry Indian stories worldwide, regional studios that trust local language and detail, and partnerships that open finance, technology and new markets. With better marketing, strong post-production, and training that lifts on-set standards, cinema can reach a forty-billion-dollar value by 2035.

Music: the soundtrack of a living civilisation

Hindustani and Carnatic traditions sit beside folk lineages, film scores and an independent scene that grows each month. The market now rests on streaming, live circuits, and direct-to-fan models; platforms give village and small-town artists pathways that once did not exist. The next decade invites bolder work: classical and jazz or electronic collaborations, film music built for global playlists, and festival routes that draw listeners to places where music began. Exports can rise quickly when rights are clear, metadata is clean, and touring circuits link cities with heritage venues.

Art, craft and handicraft: tradition as livelihood

More than seven million artisans sustain crafts in metal, wood, clay, textiles, jewellery and painting. They carry techniques learned at home, and they teach by doing, which keeps knowledge alive in families and guilds. Segments with strong pull include Banarasi and Kanjeevaram silk, Pashmina and Phulkari,

Dhokra metalwork, blue pottery, Bidri, and Madhubani. Programmes such as ODOP and GI tags help identity and pricing; digital marketplaces make reach possible; design schools and craft clusters can raise finish and consistency without dulling the hand-made character. With patient support, crafts can add significant value by 2040 while placing income in women's hands and anchoring young people in their home districts.

Literature and publishing: words that shape the day

India prints and sells in many tongues, with English titles adding reach abroad. Fiction, essays, poetry, study guides, children's books and spiritual writing all find readers; education lists remain strong; translation grows as readers seek voices from other states and countries. Digital editions widen access, while audio gives commuters and busy parents a way back into books. With care for editing quality, rights management and international fair presence, India can become a literary hub for the Global South, a place where new thought meets clear expression.

Digital and OTT platforms: a new commons

Hundreds of millions now stream shows, films, music and live events. OTT revenue is set for a long climb, helped by multilingual catalogues and low data costs. YouTube, short-video platforms and podcasts have turned many young creators into professionals. Animation, gaming and VFX add a technical spine to the creative economy, and they open careers that blend art with code. Stable rules for payments, content classification and creator contracts will keep this space healthy and fair.

Comparative global insights

Scale looks different across countries, yet influence travels in many ways. The United States builds vast franchises through film, streaming and games; South Korea shows the strength of coordinated music and drama exports; Japan carries global animation; the United Kingdom holds long traditions in music, television formats and literature. India's advantage lies in cultural variety and affordability, which speak clearly to audiences across Africa, the Middle East and Southeast Asia, while also winning steady attention in Europe and North America.

A quick global view

Country	Entertainment industry revenue (USD billion)	Global cultural influence	Key export
India	30	High in film, music, yoga and design heritage	Films, crafts, digital content
USA	700+	Dominant	Hollywood, streaming, gaming
South Korea	20	High	Music, drama, fashion
Japan	35	Strong	Anime, games
UK	60	Strong	Music, literature, TV formats

Cultural tourism and soft power

Festivals, fairs, film trails, craft markets, yoga retreats and sacred circuits bring travellers to places where culture lives. World Heritage Sites, museum quarters and riverfronts add structure; biennales and literature festivals bring new audiences to local artists; craft streets and design districts keep spending near the makers. When arts, tourism and education move together, earnings grow without stripping places of their character.

Cultural tourism opportunities

Cultural tourism type	Visitors (million)	Annual revenue (USD billion)	Potential jobs created (million)
Film tourism	10	20	1
Spiritual tourism	25	30	3
Art and festival tourism	15	25	2
Heritage and handicraft	20	30	4
Total	**70**	**105**	**10**

Policy support and future prospects

Public policy has begun to treat culture as a strategy. The Film Facilitation Office helps shoots and co-productions; cultural mapping gives visibility to artists and crafts; destination branding links events with travel calendars. The next steps are plain: strong intellectual property protection, simple finance for small studios and artisan groups, export support at global fairs and on streaming platforms, and digital literacy for makers who work far from big cities. When policy and private capital pull in the same direction, the creative economy stands alongside technology and manufacturing as a pillar of growth.

Vision 2040: India as a global cultural leader

The horizon is clear: a creative industry of nearly 100 billion dollars that adds more than three per cent to GDP, with fifty million livelihoods across film sets, stages, studios, workshops and design labs. Music and film exports can hold their own with the world's largest; cultural diplomacy through arts, yoga, and education will deepen friendships across continents. This vision treats culture as renewable energy for identity and respect; the more it is shared, the more it grows.

India's creative economy is old and young at once. It draws from epics and hand-carved motifs, then turns to cameras, consoles and code without losing its centre. When a child learns a step from a grandparent, when an artisan sells directly to a visitor, when a song crosses a border and finds a new chorus, prosperity and dignity move together. True wealth is not mined only from the earth; it is shaped in studios and workshops, written on pages, carried in melody, and shown on screens. That wealth builds confidence at home and regard abroad, turning expression into income and heritage into hope.

Creative sub-sectors: scale and goals

Creative sub-sector	2025 revenue (USD billion)	2035 target	2040 vision	Employment (million)
Film and television	20	35	45	4
Music and audio	2	8	10	1
Digital and OTT	5	15	25	3
Crafts and design	3	10	15	7
Publishing and literature	2	4	6	1
Total	**32**	**72**	**101**	**16+**

Cultural tourism potential

Cultural tourism type	Visitors (million)	Annual revenue (USD billion)	Potential jobs created (million)
Film tourism	10	20	1
Spiritual tourism	25	30	3
Art and festival tourism	15	25	2
Heritage and handicraft	20	30	4
Total	**70**	**105**	**10**

Financial and Banking Infrastructure: The Backbone of Modern India

Money fuels effort, yet confidence turns money into movement. A strong financial system gives that confidence to families, farmers, founders, and factories. In a country of 1.4 billion, with many incomes and many regions, a system that is efficient, inclusive, and digital is not a luxury; it is essential.

Across two decades, India has shifted from heavy use of cash to one of the most connected financial ecosystems on Earth. Policy reform met technological ingenuity and an energetic startup base, and the result is a stack that serves the street vendor and the stock investor with the same ease. A system that once struggled to reach the last mile now helps other nations study how to include millions through technology and simple design.

India's financial transformation: from independence to inclusion

At the birth of the Republic, formal banking touched fewer than one in ten citizens. Today, more than four in five adults hold an account, and UPI moves billions of payments month after month, at low cost and near-instant speed.

Four turns shaped this rise:

1. **Nationalisation of banks in 1969 and 1980**, which extended branches and credit into rural districts.

2. **Economic liberalisation in 1991** opened the door to private and foreign players and improved efficiency.
3. **Financial inclusion from 2014 onward**, where Jan Dhan accounts crossed five hundred million and brought households into the formal net.
4. **The digital layer from 2016 onward**, where Aadhaar, e-KYC and UPI fused identity, account, and payment into one user journey.

Together, these moves built one of the widest bases for financial access anywhere, and they continue to deepen reach each year.

The current banking landscape

India's banking map includes public sector banks, private banks, foreign banks, cooperative banks, regional rural banks, and young payment banks. Public institutions carry reach and trust. Private and foreign banks bring speed, product variety, and service depth. The task ahead is balance, so that inclusion and profitability move in step.

Banking mix and strengths

Bank type	Number of institutions	Market share (%)	Key strengths
Public sector banks	12	60	Government backing, deep rural presence
Private sector banks	22	30	Efficiency, product innovation, service
Foreign banks	45+	6	Global expertise, niche lending
Cooperative and regional banks	1,500+	4	Local access, microcredit support

These institutions together manage deposits of roughly USD 2.5 trillion and loans near USD 1.8 trillion, which form the base that supports growth across sectors.

The rise of fintech: India's digital revolution

India now hosts thousands of fintech firms across payments, lending, insurance, wealth, and cross-border flows. Investment has been steady, and several firms have reached scale with sound unit economics. The centrepiece is UPI, which enables account-to-account payments through a mobile interface in seconds, at nearly zero user cost. In 2025, UPI processed more than fifteen billion transactions monthly with values above USD 400 billion, and similar rails now appear in partner countries.

Key fintech segments in India

Segment	Market size 2025 (USD billion)	Growth rate (%)	Examples
Digital payments	70	20	UPI, Paytm, PhonePe
Digital lending	25	30	KreditBee, MoneyTap
Insurtech	15	25	Policybazaar, Acko
Wealthtech	10	22	Zerodha, Groww
Blockchain and Web3	5	35	Polygon, CoinDCX
Total	**125**	**26 (avg)**	–

Fintech has turned the smartphone into a bank branch, a remittance desk, an investment portal, and an insurance counter, all in one hand.

Financial Inclusion: Empowering the Unbanked

Gaps remain between city and village, and between formal access and effective use. Rural India holds most of the people, yet contributes a smaller slice of deposits. Policy focuses on closing this divide with accounts, credit, insurance, and literacy.

Key drivers:

- **Jan Dhan Yojana**, with five hundred million plus accounts since 2014.
- **PM Mudra Yojana**, with over USD 200 billion in loans to small entrepreneurs.

- **Self-Help Groups**, which organise more than eighty million women for savings and microcredit.
- **Microfinance institutions**, which carry last-mile credit to households.

With digital literacy and strong grievance redressal, full inclusion by 2035 can lift tens of millions from poverty and spark local enterprise.

Stock markets and capital formation

BSE and NSE rank among the busiest markets worldwide. By 2025, listed value crossed USD 4 trillion, and retail participation grew through low-fee brokers and easy-to-use apps. More than 120 million Indians now invest in equities or mutual funds, which spreads wealth creation beyond large cities.

Comparative stock market view

Country	Market capitalisation (USD trillion)	Retail participation (%)	Primary industries
USA	46	35	Technology, healthcare, finance
China	12	20	Manufacturing, technology
India	4	15	IT, banking, energy
Japan	6	10	Electronics, automobiles
UK	3	25	Finance, energy

With domestic savings, pension reform, and steady foreign flows, India can move toward USD 10 trillion in market value by 2035.

Insurance, pensions, and financial security

Coverage remains the next big step. Life cover reaches roughly a third of citizens, and health cover reaches roughly a fifth. Programmes such as Ayushman Bharat, PM Suraksha Bima Yojana, and Atal Pension Yojana expand the safety net. If private channels and digital distribution scale wisely, insurance can reach USD 1 trillion by 2040, while also supplying long-term capital to infrastructure and research.

Financial technology and the blockchain horizon

Blockchain adds auditability and speed to flows where trust and proof matter. The Reserve Bank's Digital Rupee pilots test a central bank digital currency for wholesale and retail uses. Early opportunities include clean delivery of subsidies, faster remittances, land record integrity, supply-chain traceability, and small-ticket lending with better risk signals. With prudent scale-up and clear rules, the contribution to GDP by 2035 can reach USD 100–150 billion.

Global comparisons and lessons

Open banking in Brazil, mobile money in Kenya, deep markets in the United States, and scaled platforms in China all offer cues. India brings a different mix: public digital rails, simple KYC, and a vibrant private layer.

Digital banking and key lessons

Country	Digital banking penetration (%)	Key strength	Lesson for India
India	80	Inclusive, mobile-first stack	Expand rural credit access
USA	95	Mature fintech with deep capital markets	Strengthen risk management
Kenya	70	Mobile money success	Join microfinance with digital tools
China	90	Large-scale digital ecosystem	Regulate market power while innovating
Brazil	75	Open banking leadership	Enhance interoperability

India Stack shows how public infrastructure and private entrepreneurship can lift access at a population scale.

Challenges in The Financial Sector

Clear obstacles remain:

1. Rural credit scarcity where collateral is thin and risk data is weak.
2. Non-performing assets are in parts of the public banking system.
3. Limited supplies of long-term capital for roads, power, and urban services.
4. Complex regulation that slows product design and testing.
5. Cybersecurity risks as transaction counts rise.

Answering these calls for coherent policy, stronger supervision, open yet responsible data use, and a steady push on governance.

Vision 2040: financial powerhouse of the Global South

By 2040, India can carry a USD 10–12 trillion economy with financial services contributing more than a quarter of value added. Every citizen can be banked, insured, and digitally connected. Fintech exports can cross USD 100 billion each year. A trusted Digital Rupee can support cross-border settlement. Green finance can fund renewable energy, efficient logistics, and climate-ready cities.

This future measures success in dignity as much as in yield, since savings, credit, insurance, and investment give people tools to plan, to build, and to dream with confidence.

From a narrow colonial base to a wide digital network, India has rebuilt finance to serve scale and diversity. Banks, NBFCs, microcredit, mutual funds, UPI, and early blockchain rails now sit on one canvas from farms to factories, from research labs to classrooms. Finance no longer lives in a distant district office. It stands in every hand, in every village, and in every small shop that scans a QR code for payment.

A strong financial spine does more than push growth; it carries the hopes of a billion people and spreads opportunity outward so that prosperity can be shared.

Headline indicators

Indicator	2025	2035 target	2040 vision
Financial inclusion, adults with accounts (%)	80	95	100
UPI monthly transactions (billion)	15	25	40
Total deposits (USD trillion)	2.5	5	8
Fintech market value (USD billion)	125	250	400
Insurance penetration (%)	35	60	80

Employment and GDP contribution by segment

Key segment	2025 employment (million)	2040 employment (million)	GDP contribution by 2040 (USD trillion)
Banking and NBFCs	3.5	6	2.5
Fintech and digital finance	1.5	4	1.0
Insurance and pensions	1.0	2	0.8
Capital markets and wealth management	0.5	1	0.7
Total	**6.5**	**13**	**5.0+**

Startup and Entrepreneurship Potential: The Engine of Innovation

Enterprise gives shape to ideas. It turns creativity into commerce, ambition into livelihoods, and hope into working models that serve people. For a country with one of the youngest populations on Earth, entrepreneurship forms the base of a self-reliant and globally competitive future.

Over the last decade, India moved from a services-heavy posture to an innovation-led engine. What began with a handful of technology pioneers in Bengaluru and Gurugram now reaches every region and sector, from agritech teams in small towns to AI research ventures in Tier-2 cities.

The Rise of The Indian Startup Ecosystem

India stands among the largest startup ecosystems in the world, alongside the United States and China. In 2025, the country hosted more than 120,000 active startups, with over 120 unicorns, together contributing nearly five per cent of GDP. A new generation chose to build at home, serving global markets from Indian soil.

Four drivers powered this surge:

1. **Policy support.** Startup India, Digital India, and Make in India reduced entry barriers and opened funding routes.
2. **Digital rails.** Fast internet, low data prices, and UPI placed technology within reach across districts.
3. **Investment depth.** Venture funds, angel networks, and public programmes such as SIDBI and the Startup India Fund expanded early and growth capital.
4. **Global reach.** Indian teams sell to international clients, export digital services, and attract overseas investors.

Comparative global perspective

Scale and speed make clear how far the ecosystem has travelled, while the pattern remains adapted to Indian realities of frugality, diversity, and inclusion.

Global snapshot of startup hubs (2025)

Country	Active startups	Annual funding (USD bn)	Unicorns	Key strength
USA	600,000+	350	600+	Advanced R&D, deep capital access
China	200,000+	100	300+	Manufacturing innovation, state support
India	**120,000+**	**45+**	**120+**	Youth talent, digital ecosystem
UK	70,000	30	50	Fintech, creative industries
Israel	10,000	25	30	Deep-tech, defence innovation

Startup Sectors Powering India's Future

New firms now appear in nearly every part of the economy, often solving long-standing problems through design and code.

- **Technology and IT.** SaaS, AI, cloud, cyber security. Examples: Zoho, Freshworks, Druva. Outcome: global B2B leadership.
- **Fintech.** Payments, lending, insurtech. Examples: Razorpay, PhonePe, Zerodha. Outcome: inclusion and efficiency.

- **Healthtech.** Telemedicine, diagnostics. Examples: Practo, PharmEasy, HealthifyMe. Outcome: affordable care.
- **Edtech.** E-learning, skills. Examples: Byju's, Unacademy, Vedantu. Outcome: workforce upskilling.
- **Agritech.** Precision farming, market linkage. Examples: Ninjacart, DeHaat, AgroStar. Outcome: higher farmer income.
- **Clean energy.** Solar, EV, batteries. Examples: Ola Electric, Ather, ReNew Power. Outcome: greener growth.
- **Deep-tech.** Robotics, quantum, aerospace. Examples: Agnikul, Bellatrix, Pixxel. Outcome: strategic capability.
- **Tourism and culture.** Experience platforms and heritage tech. Examples: Thrillophilia, MakeMyTrip. Outcome: soft-power lift.

More than half of new ventures now emerge from Tier-2 and Tier-3 cities, which spreads opportunity beyond metros.

Economic Impact of the Startup Revolution

Young firms already reshape the labour market and the export basket.

- Direct employment: above 10 million across formal roles and the gig economy.
- Indirect employment: 20–25 million across logistics, manufacturing, and services.
- GDP contribution: trending toward 8–10 per cent by 2035, from five per cent in 2025.

- Innovation exports: software and digital services are worth more than USD 50 billion each year.

If fully supported, startups could add USD 1.5–2.0 trillion to GDP by 2040.

Startup impact forecast

Indicator	2025	2030	2040 (potential)
Active startups	120,000	200,000	350,000
Unicorns	120	250	500
Jobs created (million)	10	20	35
GDP contribution (%)	5	7	10
Startup funding (USD bn)	45	100	250

Women and Social Entrepreneurs: The inclusive edge

A distinctive strength of this movement is inclusion. More than one in five new ventures are founded or co-founded by women, supported by platforms such as Naari Startups, SHE Capital, and WE Hub. Social enterprises blend profit with purpose in areas such as rural livelihoods, clean water, and education. Examples include Selco, Araku Coffee, and Bare Necessities. By 2040, women-led and social ventures could form 30 to 35 per cent of the ecosystem, giving growth a balanced, mission-driven character.

Role of government and policy in fostering innovation

A supportive framework underpins momentum:

- **Startup India (2016).** Simplified registration, tax benefits, and a ₹10,000 crore fund.
- **Digital India.** Broadband, cloud, and public digital goods.
- **Atal Innovation Mission.** Incubators in schools and universities.
- **PLI schemes.** Tailwinds for manufacturing-led ventures.
- **State policies.** Kerala, Gujarat, Telangana and others built strong local systems.
- **Regulatory sandboxes.** SEBI and RBI allow live testing in fintech and blockchain, lowering early compliance burdens while keeping safeguards.

Startups and global expansion

Indian companies now scale across continents. Examples include Freshworks on NASDAQ, Zoho serving more than 180 countries, OYO operating in 80-plus nations, and BYJU'S building a global learner base. By 2035, combined overseas revenue could cross USD 300 billion, turning founders into ambassadors of Indian innovation.

Startup challenges and the path ahead

Progress is real, yet hurdles remain:

1. Early-stage capital gaps in several regions.
2. Overlap across regulators complicates compliance.

3. Retention challenges in specialised roles across AI, biotech, and hardware.
4. Logistics constraints and slow patent enforcement.
5. Profitability strain after rapid scale-up.

A **National Innovation Grid** can link research labs, industry partners, investors, and universities, easing the journey from prototype to product and from product to global market.

The Future: India as a Global Innovation Hub

Growth vectors for the next wave:

- **AI and robotics.** Rich data ecosystems suit model development and applied AI.
- **Biotechnology and pharma-tech.** Strong medical base supports personalised medicine and affordable diagnostics.
- **Clean-tech and circular economy.** Startups design climate solutions and create green jobs.
- **Space-tech.** Private teams extend launch and satellite services alongside ISRO.
- **Rural tech and agri-innovation.** Local solutions scale across the Global South.

This mix keeps the model technologically bold, socially relevant, and export-ready.

Vision 2040: the entrepreneurial nation

By 2040, India can host more than 350,000 startups and 500 or more unicorns with a combined value of near USD 2 trillion. Direct employment can reach

35–40 million, with many more roles in allied services. Founders in Kochi, coders in Indore, designers in Shillong, and scientists in Hyderabad can build together for India and the world.

When policy stability meets private courage and public digital infrastructure, business becomes a national habit, and innovation becomes daily work.

✦ ✦ ✦

4

Stakeholders and Their Contributions to Make India Developed

"Alone we can do so little; together we can do so much."
– Helen Keller

India's progress depends on everyone who calls it home. Turning a developing country into a developed one cannot be the job of a single institution or a few policymakers. It is a shared effort that needs the participation of millions of people, each contributing in their own way. The work of building a nation belongs as much to the teacher in a small town as to the policymaker in Delhi. Every role matters.

The term *stakeholder* in development refers to any individual, group, or institution whose decisions, resources, or actions influence the country's progress. India's development cannot rest on the shoulders of the government or the private sector alone. It is a collective journey that needs the energy, wisdom, and will of everyone: citizens, companies, farmers, teachers, entrepreneurs, civil servants, and international partners.

When all these forces align, progress becomes stronger and more sustainable.

India's diversity gives it great strength but also presents complex challenges. A country with over 1.4 billion people, hundreds of languages, and countless cultures cannot grow through one approach or one idea. Progress comes when all parts of society move together. Economic growth, social equality, environmental care, and good governance must advance side by side. Development gains meaning only when every citizen feels seen, supported, and involved in shaping the country's direction.

A nation grows when all its stakeholders act with shared purpose. The government, private enterprise, civil society, educators, farmers, the media, and ordinary citizens all play connected roles. Even global partners contribute by sharing technology, expertise, and investment. When these parts work together, growth becomes continuous and inclusive.

The government carries the first responsibility. It sets the direction and builds the systems that others depend on. Policies, infrastructure, and regulations form the base on which the rest of the economy stands. A well-governed state ensures that rules are fair, opportunities reach both cities and villages, and services work for every citizen.

India has made major strides through large national missions. Clean water has reached rural homes through the Jal Jeevan Mission. Health coverage has expanded through Ayushman Bharat. Affordable housing, digital banking, and electrification have transformed millions of lives. Programs that link Aadhaar, Jan Dhan, and mobile services have reduced leakages and created inclusion.

The government also drives investment in infrastructure and innovation. Freight corridors, expressways, ports, and airports have reduced travel time and improved trade. Digital systems like UPI and DigiLocker have made payments and documentation fast and transparent. When public institutions work with clarity, growth begins to reach the ground.

The private sector powers the nation's economy. It generates employment, builds industries, and introduces technology. From large companies to small enterprises and start-ups, private effort creates opportunities and moves ideas into action.

India's businesses have grown rapidly in recent decades. The IT sector leads the world in software services. The pharmaceutical industry supplies affordable medicine globally. Renewable energy, automobiles, and manufacturing have all expanded. Start-ups have turned innovation into practical solutions for education, healthcare, logistics, and finance.

Companies have also taken an active role in community work through social responsibility programs. Many have invested in schools, hospitals, and skilling centres in rural areas. Public-private partnerships have delivered clean energy, affordable housing, and better transport networks. The private sector shows how enterprise, guided by ethics and vision, can build both profit and public good.

Civil society gives development a human touch. Non-governmental organizations, community groups, and volunteers connect policy with people. They reach where government services sometimes struggle to go and ensure that progress includes the vulnerable.

Across India, social organizations have changed lives in education, health, and equality. The Akshaya Patra Foundation feeds millions of schoolchildren. SEWA has empowered women workers across sectors. Pratham continues to improve basic learning in public schools. These examples show how service and compassion can move a society forward.

Civil society also helps democracy stay strong. It gives citizens a platform to speak, question, and collaborate. When local communities participate in their own development, from managing water resources to running self-help groups, progress becomes lasting and inclusive.

Education builds the foundation for every other form of progress. Schools and universities shape the citizens who will lead industries, government, and research. India's long tradition of learning continues through its modern institutions. The IITs, IIMs, AIIMS, and many state universities have built a generation of global professionals.

Yet, true progress in education depends on how deep quality reaches. Every school must give children a chance to think freely and develop skills that connect to real work. Teachers need training and resources, and students need encouragement to innovate.

Investment in research is equally vital. The more a country invests in science, technology, and innovation, the more it strengthens its future. Collaboration between universities and industries can produce new ideas for healthcare, agriculture, and clean energy. Education, when it moves beyond theory and serves practical needs, becomes the strongest form of national wealth.

Media carries the pulse of a democracy. It connects people to information, holds institutions accountable, and builds awareness. A responsible media informs rather than divides, and helps citizens make decisions with clarity.

India's media space is vast and vibrant. Newspapers, television, digital outlets, and community radio reach millions every day. Campaigns that promote health, environmental awareness, or citizen rights have changed public attitudes and improved policies. When the media uses its influence responsibly, it strengthens both trust and transparency.

Farmers sustain the nation. They feed the people, supply industries, and support half of the workforce. The health of agriculture shapes the health of the country.

The Green Revolution turned India into a food-secure nation. Now, the goal is to make farming sustainable and profitable. Farmers need access to modern equipment, irrigation, insurance, and direct markets. Better roads, cold storage, and processing facilities can prevent waste and raise incomes. Digital platforms are helping farmers connect to buyers and learn about prices, weather, and technology.

When agriculture grows with technology and care for the environment, rural India becomes the base of a strong economy.

Every citizen is a stakeholder in the nation's progress. Paying taxes, voting responsibly, following the law, and protecting public property are basic duties that build a nation from within. Development grows stronger when citizens see themselves as partners, not spectators.

Community participation brings powerful results. People who take initiative to clean neighbourhoods, save water, plant trees, or volunteer in schools add to national progress in lasting ways. A country's strength reflects the discipline and empathy of its people.

India's growth is linked to the world. Partnerships with other nations and global organizations bring knowledge, technology, and investment. Cooperation in areas such as renewable energy, trade, and digital innovation expands opportunity for all.

India's collaboration with Japan has built industrial corridors. Its partnership with France has strengthened solar energy initiatives. Relations with the United States and Europe have encouraged research and entrepreneurship. Global institutions like the World Bank and the Asian Development Bank have supported large-scale infrastructure projects.

India also contributes to global progress. From sending vaccines to countries in need to sharing digital frameworks with developing nations, it plays a leadership role that reflects both strength and generosity.

Development is the sum of many efforts moving in the same direction. Governments design the framework. Businesses build engines of growth. Civil society ensures inclusion. Schools create knowledge. Media spreads awareness. Farmers feed the nation. Citizens uphold values. International partners bring learning and partnership.

Each of these efforts matters. When combined, they form a national movement that drives India forward. A developed India will be one where everyone contributes and everyone benefits; where progress is measured not only in income but in opportunity, dignity, and shared pride.

The journey toward that goal has already begun, powered by millions of hands working with a single purpose: *to see India rise with strength, equality, and grace.*

Government: The Guiding Force

A nation grows when its government leads with clarity, consistency, and care. The government carries the duty of setting direction, creating systems that work, and making sure that development reaches every person. It turns collective dreams into national goals and national goals into everyday change.

India's story of progress is large and layered. Every decision, from laying a road to reforming education, connects with the lives of millions. A government that listens, plans with foresight, and delivers with honesty gives strength to citizens, industry, and communities alike.

Policy That Shapes Growth

Policies turn ideas into action. They build bridges between planning and people. When framed well and implemented with purpose, they touch every aspect of life, from learning in a village school to healthcare in a city hospital.

Education stands at the heart of development. It shapes the skill and confidence of a generation. Recent reforms focus on making learning practical and accessible. The National Education Policy has brought new energy to schools and universities. Skill development programs and vocational training centres are preparing youth for real work. STEM education is growing in schools, and scholarships are opening doors for students who previously had limited access.

Area	Government Focus	Visible Outcome
Schooling	NEP 2020, Samagra Shiksha	Better classrooms and broader learning
Skills	Skill India, PMKVY	Employment readiness among youth
Research	National Research Foundation	Support for innovation in higher education
Equity	Mid-Day Meal, Beti Bachao Beti Padhao	Better nutrition and gender inclusion

Healthcare has moved to the centre of policy. Programs such as Ayushman Bharat and the National Health Mission aim to bring medical care to every family. Vaccination drives, public health campaigns, and digital health records are improving access. Rural health centres now reach deeper into remote regions, and telemedicine connects doctors to patients without travel.

Area	Government Focus	Visible Outcome
Access	Ayushman Bharat	Free or low-cost care for families
Rural Services	National Health Mission	Hospitals closer to villages
Prevention	Immunisation, sanitation	Healthier children and communities
Technology	Digital Health Mission	Online records and teleconsultation

Industry and trade provide the fuel for employment and innovation. Reforms in taxation, trade, and enterprise registration have simplified how businesses function. Start-up India, Make in India, and production-linked incentives have created confidence among entrepreneurs. Focusing on small and medium industries supports self-employment and local economies.

Area	Government Focus	Visible Outcome
Manufacturing	Make in India, PLI	Expansion in local production
Start-ups	Start-up India	New jobs and fresh ideas
MSMEs	Easy credit, e-marketplaces	Growth for smaller businesses
Exports	Logistics and customs reforms	Faster movement of goods

Infrastructure gives shape to progress. Roads, railways, housing, and digital networks connect every part of the country. Projects such as Bharatmala, Sagarmala, and Smart Cities Mission are transforming how people travel and live. Rural electrification, affordable housing, and broadband access are helping millions join the national economy.

Sector	Key Programs	Impact on Daily Life
Transport	Bharatmala, Metro Expansion	Faster travel and trade
Energy	Renewable Energy Missions	Reliable and cleaner power
Housing	PM Awas Yojana	Secure homes for families
Digital	BharatNet, Digital India	Access to online services

A government policy gains its real value when it improves daily life, when it gives a farmer irrigation, a student a teacher, and a worker a skill.

Governance That Builds Confidence

Policies need systems that work. Governance is where vision turns into reality. When public services are honest and efficient, trust grows naturally.

India's digital governance has changed how people interact with the state. Aadhaar, Jan Dhan accounts, and direct benefit transfers have reduced delays and misuse. Pensions, scholarships, and subsidies now reach citizens without middlemen. This has restored faith in institutions and improved everyday convenience.

Local governments bring administration closer to the people. Panchayats and municipalities can act faster because they know local needs. Programs like the Gram Panchayat Development Plan have given villages more control over their budgets. Empowering local bodies ensures that governance reflects real needs instead of distant plans.

Transparency is another strength. Online tendering, open project dashboards, and public grievance systems make the government accountable. People can track where money goes and how projects move. This visibility strengthens participation and responsibility.

Law and justice form the core of public safety. Faster courts, digital filings, and legal reforms protect citizens' rights and make business more reliable. Security and fairness give citizens the confidence to invest their time and effort in building a better future.

Research and Innovation for a Self-Reliant Future

Innovation drives progress that lasts. India's public investment in research has helped farmers, scientists, and entrepreneurs find new solutions. From developing space technology to designing vaccines, Indian researchers are shaping the nation's future.

Government-supported institutions like ISRO, DRDO, and CSIR have built models of excellence. Agricultural research improves yields and reduces losses. Renewable energy research is moving India closer to clean power goals. Technology incubators and innovation hubs encourage students and start-ups to take ideas to the market.

Field	Key Program	Outcome
Space and Science	ISRO Missions	Global recognition for research excellence
Agriculture	ICAR Research	Higher crop yields and sustainable farming
Energy	National Solar Mission	Growth in renewable energy generation
Health	Biotechnology Innovation	Affordable vaccines and healthcare products

Public-private partnerships are vital in this process. When industry collaborates with universities, research moves faster and benefits reach people sooner.

Social Welfare and Inclusion

A strong nation uplifts everyone. Welfare programs create safety and dignity for those who need support.

Employment schemes such as MGNREGA provide income in rural areas. Affordable housing programs have given families security and stability. Financial inclusion through Jan Dhan accounts and direct transfers has brought millions into the formal economy. Women's empowerment programs encourage education, health, and entrepreneurship.

Area	Government Focus	Visible Result
Rural Work	MGNREGA	Steady income for households
Food Security	PDS, Mid-Day Meal	Reduced hunger and improved nutrition
Women's Welfare	Ujjwala, Beti Bachao	Better health and opportunity
Financial Access	Jan Dhan Yojana	Inclusion in formal banking

True inclusion comes when every person feels seen and supported. Welfare programs matter most when they create independence rather than dependence, when they give citizens the means to shape their own lives.

Vision for the Future

Governance must plan for the present and prepare for tomorrow. India's government continues to build a vision that looks ahead to a changing world. Digital India connects services and people. Make in India creates jobs and industry. Atmanirbhar Bharat encourages local innovation and self-reliance.

Climate policies and renewable energy projects protect the environment for future generations. Smart city plans make urban life efficient and sustainable. Long-term missions in education, energy, and research ensure that growth does not fade but matures over time.

National Vision	Purpose	Broader Outcome
Digital India	Universal connectivity	Access to knowledge and governance
Make in India	Strengthen local production	Job creation and self-sufficiency
Atmanirbhar Bharat	Economic independence	Innovation-led growth
Renewable Energy Mission	Sustainable development	Cleaner air and long-term stability

The government's purpose is larger than administration. It is the guide that turns effort into impact. When public service is grounded in vision and accountability, it inspires confidence in citizens and encourages every sector to work with unity.

India's rise depends on the quality of its governance, policies that serve, systems that deliver, and leaders who act with purpose. When these align, the nation's growth becomes more than an ambition. It becomes a shared achievement carried by every citizen.

Private Sector: Engine of Growth

India moves forward when enterprise turns ideas into work. The private sector brings energy, capital, and skill to the nation's table.

Government frames the rules. Business builds on them.

Together they turn plans into factories, farms into value chains, and talent into livelihoods. What follows is how Indian enterprise powers growth in ways people can see and feel.

Building Industry And Technology

From the shop floor to the cloud, companies raise productivity and widen opportunities. Car makers and auto part suppliers keep supply chains busy across states. Textile units in Tiruppur and Surat send garments worldwide. Pharma hubs in Hyderabad and Ahmedabad produce affordable medicines. Electronics parks in Noida and Sriperumbudur assemble devices for global brands.

Technology firms write code that runs banks, hospitals, and governments. Fintech brings payments and credit to small vendors. Healthtech connects doctors to patients in towns and villages. Renewable energy firms install solar parks in Rajasthan and wind farms in Gujarat and Tamil Nadu, cutting costs and creating green jobs. Startups build AI tools, logistics networks, and agritech platforms that help farmers plan crops, reduce waste, and reach better markets.

Industry-education partnerships matter here. When companies work with ITIs, polytechnics, and universities, students gain hands-on skills and internships that lead to jobs. Apprenticeship programs give youth a first step into the workplace and give firms a pipeline of trained talent.

Partnering With The Public Sector

Public-private partnerships turn large goals into delivered projects. In transport, private expertise helps build and operate metro lines while the government ensures access and safety. In health, diagnostic chains and hospitals expand their reach under public insurance. In power, private developers add renewable capacity while grid upgrades come through public investment. Urban water, waste, and street lighting improve when city bodies and operators share clear contracts and service standards.

Well-structured PPPs do three things. They bring speed, they spread risk, and they keep service outcomes in focus. People care less about who owns an asset and more about whether the train runs on time and the clinic is open with staff and supplies.

Creating Jobs And Widening Inclusion

The most visible contribution of the enterprise is work. Large firms employ directly and through supplier networks. Small and medium enterprises employ locally, often in places where other options are few. Startups create roles in design, data, sales, and support. Rural and semi-urban clusters in food processing, handloom, leather, furniture, and tourism support families and keep skills alive.

Entrepreneurship lifts inclusion. Women-led self-help groups run micro-units for food, garments, and crafts. Platforms bring their products to national markets. Social enterprises train youth from low-income backgrounds and place them in steady jobs. When credit is linked to digital records and repayment history, first-time borrowers build trust and grow.

Responsibility That Builds Trust

Corporate Social Responsibility has turned many balance sheets into community projects. Companies support schools, skilling centres, and health camps. They fund clean water, sanitation, and local sports. Environmental projects replant trees, restore lakes, and improve waste management.

Sustainability is now a core business. Plants adopt energy-efficient processes. Supply chains reduce waste. Factories install solar rooftops and switch to cleaner fuels. Fair wages, safe workplaces, and strong grievance systems keep people at the centre. Ethical practice is good business. It lowers risk and raises pride among employees and customers.

Innovating For India And The World

Investment in research turns effort into an advantage. Indian firms file patents in materials, pharma, automotive components, and electronics. Collaboration with global partners brings new techniques and markets. Exports of software, engineering services, chemicals, textiles, and auto parts carry the India story to over a hundred countries.

Venture capital and angel networks back founders who solve Indian problems at Indian price points. Mobile payments at scale, low-cost diagnostics, rural e-commerce, and multilingual education tools show how innovation can serve both growth and inclusion.

Clearing Hurdles And Seizing New Ground

Challenges remain. Small firms seek simpler rules, faster permissions, and reliable power. Access to patient capital is a hurdle for technology hardware and deep science. Logistics in some corridors need better first and last-mile links.

Reforms are opening doors. Digital portals cut paperwork. Production-linked incentives anchor new factories. Freight corridors reduce the time to port. New sectors are rising fast. Green hydrogen, battery storage, semiconductors, space-tech, and biotech offer room for Indian firms to lead with scale and quality.

When an enterprise thrives with integrity, the nation gains. Jobs grow, exports rise, and skills deepen. Cities get new services. Villages find new buyers. Young people see a future they can shape with their own hands.

India's private sector has the power to turn this decade into a decade of building. Build products that last. Build companies that train. Build supply chains that pay on time. Build technology that includes. With each of these, India moves from potential to performance, and from performance to pride.

Civil Society: The Heartbeat of Democracy

Enterprises build, governments enable, and civil society makes sure progress reaches every person. This is where citizens stand up for what is right, fill gaps on the ground, and keep every institution honest. In a country as large as India, this voice is essential.

Civil society includes NGOs, community groups, cooperatives, professional bodies, volunteer networks, and many individual citizens. Together, they turn concern into action. They teach where schools are weak, treat where clinics are far, protect rivers and forests, and speak for those who do not get heard. They help growth stay humane and accountable.

Advocacy and accountability

Civil society watches how power is used. It studies policies, checks spending, and reports where delivery fails. Research notes and public campaigns bring missing issues into view. Court petitions and audits follow when needed. This work improves programmes and protects public money.

Environmental groups review large projects and ask for safeguards. Education and health groups track outcomes, not announcements. Workers' groups help improve safety and pay. When citizens see facts presented calmly and clearly, trust rises and action follows.

Social Welfare And Grassroots Work

Across districts, local organisations run schools after hours, host adult literacy, and fund scholarships. Mobile health units bring doctors to remote hamlets. Maternal care, vaccination support, and sanitation drives reduce illness. In many places, community kitchens and nutrition camps keep children in school and mothers healthy.

Skill centres teach tailoring, plumbing, electrical work, and basic coding. Self-help groups learn accounting and market access. Microcredit and mentoring turn small ideas into steady income. Each small step adds security to a family and dignity to work.

A strong democracy needs informed citizens. Civil society explains rights and duties in simple words. Voter helpdesks guide first-time voters. Ward meetings discuss water, waste, lighting, and safety. Volunteers help with disaster relief and public campaigns on road safety, hygiene, and energy saving.

When citizens participate, local bodies plan better. A village that meets monthly to review water use and school attendance often solves problems faster than any distant office.

Partnerships That Scale Impact

Civil society works best when it works with others. With government helps design and deliver programmes in schools, clinics, and skills. With companies, it uses CSR funds to run hostels, libraries, and training centres. With universities, it measures results and improves methods.

Good partnerships set clear goals, timelines, and reviews. Each partner adds its strength. The state brings reach and rules. Companies bring management and technology. Local groups bring trust and knowledge of the ground. Together, they deliver more for less cost.

Human rights and social justice

Groups that defend rights keep the nation true to its Constitution. They help women access police and courts. They support children who need protection. They work with persons with disabilities to secure access and employment. They document bonded labour, trafficking, and discrimination, and push for remedies.

This work is patient and often quiet. It prevents harm and restores dignity. A society that protects the weak grows stronger at its core.

Civic Movements And Social Innovation

India has a long record of citizens coming together to solve shared problems. City groups revive lakes. Farmer collectives reduce input costs and raise prices for produce. Youth networks run clean-up drives and reading clubs. Social enterprises use simple tech to deliver health checks, tutoring, and farm advisories through phones.

These ideas spread when they work. A lake revived in one city becomes a model for another. A rural reading camp becomes a state programme. Innovation moves from a lane to a district because it proves itself in people's lives.

The Hurdles To Overcome

Civil society faces real constraints. Small groups struggle with funds and trained staff. Compliance can be complex. Coordination between groups is often weak, which leads to overlap. Some face safety concerns when they work on sensitive issues.

Credibility matters. Clean accounts, public reports, and community boards help build trust. Training in management and data use lifts quality. Digital tools reduce cost and widen reach.

Digital platforms allow a local group to raise funds from across the country. Young professionals want to volunteer their skills on weekends. Companies seek partners who can deliver outcomes in education, health, and skilling. Government missions invite proposals for last-mile delivery.

Linking these pieces can multiply impact. A district coalition that meets quarterly and shares data can cover more ground with the same resources. Partnerships with colleges can add interns to projects during term breaks. Clear outcome targets keep everyone focused on results that matter to citizens.

Civil society keeps India's growth **humane**. It reminds every system that the goal is a child who learns, a patient who heals, a worker who earns, a street that stays safe, and a river that runs clean. It brings courage to public life and partnership to daily work.

Individuals: The Smallest but Vital Unit

Civil society gives voice to communities. The next step belongs to each of us. A nation rises when its people choose to learn, work with pride, care for neighbours, and stand up for what is right. Institutions set the stage, yet the performance comes from citizens who act every day.

Learning And Skills That Open Doors

Education changes a life and then changes a family. It builds confidence and choice. Children who read well in the early classes handle every subject better. Teens who work on projects in labs understand how knowledge turns into tools. Adults who upskill through vocational courses or online programs keep pace with new jobs.

India offers many paths. ITIs and polytechnics train technicians and artisans. Online platforms teach coding, data analysis, sales, accounting, and design. Renewable energy, healthcare support, and logistics are growing fast and need certified workers. When a nurse learns to handle new equipment, when a technician earns a welding certificate, when a coder completes a cloud course, incomes rise, and teams perform better.

Learning is also a characteristic. Schools and homes teach honesty, service, teamwork, and care for public spaces. These values hold a society together when times are tough.

Personal learning toolkit

- Read daily.
- Practice one skill that earns.

- Finish one certificate each year.
- Teach one person what you know.

Citizenship In Action

Nations thrive when citizens carry out their duties with pride. Paying taxes, following the law, voting with thought, and respecting public property turn ideals into outcomes. A drain stays clean when each lane keeps litter off the street. A ward stays safe when families know their beat officer and use helplines. A school improves when parents join its management committee and ask for the basics on time.

Local forums matter. Ward meetings, gram sabhas, and residents' gatherings set priorities that fit local needs. A streetlight request, a broken footpath, a water schedule, a library hour, and a bus stop near a clinic. Small wins add up when people show up.

Ways to participate

- Attend one local meeting each quarter.
- Report civic issues through official apps.
- Join a neighbourhood clean-up day.
- Support a public school or clinic near you.

Building Through Entrepreneurship

A person with an idea and the courage to try creates work for many. Small businesses and start-ups turn needs into services. A dairy collective raises incomes. A tailoring unit supplies uniforms to nearby schools. A solar installer lights up village homes. A food processing unit buys from local farms and sells to city stores. Social enterprises solve problems and earn sustainably.

Government programmes and incubators now help with mentoring, seed funds, and market access. District industries centres, MSME portals, and e-commerce platforms lower barriers. Experienced founders guide first-time entrepreneurs so they avoid common mistakes.

Steps that help a new venture

- Start with one paying customer.
- Keep accounts clean from day one.
- Pay suppliers on time to build trust.
- Train and retain two apprentices each year.

Giving Time And Heart

A society grows generous when people give time, skills, and resources. Volunteers teach reading after school. Doctors and nurses run weekend camps. Lawyers help with documents for the poor. Engineers design low-cost water filters for villages. Alumni adopt classrooms. Retirees mentor youth and coach sports. A few hours a month change many lives.

Philanthropy also matters. Small monthly donations to proven groups create steady support for nutrition, scholarships, hostels for girls, and disability care. Collective giving through friends and workplaces multiplies impact.

Simple ways to serve

- Read with two children each week.
- Donate a small amount each month to a trusted cause.
- Share your professional skills with one organisation.
- Plant and care for two trees in your street or school.

Health And Well-Being

A healthy person gives more at home and at work. Regular exercise, balanced food, adequate sleep, and preventive checks reduce disease. Vaccinations keep families safe. Clean hands and safe water stop illness. Mental health needs attention, too. Talk to family. Seek help when stress builds. Support friends who need care.

Workplaces can help by offering health checks, sports clubs, and counselling. Schools can teach nutrition and hygiene early. Communities can organise yoga mornings, walking groups, and blood donation drives.

Daily health basics

- Move for 30 minutes.
- Drink safe water.
- Eat fresh and moderate.
- Sleep well and on time.
- Speak up when you need support.

Caring For The Environment

Every home can save water and energy. Fix leaks. Use buckets where possible. Turn off appliances. Segregate waste. Compost wet waste for plants. Carry a reusable bottle and bag. Choose public transport when available. Support lake and river clean-ups. Encourage rainwater harvesting in your building. Ask your workplace to switch to LED lighting and rooftop solar where feasible.

Farmers can use micro-irrigation, soil testing, and crop rotation to conserve resources and protect yield. Schools can run eco-clubs and nurture kitchen gardens. Small acts across millions of homes bring large results.

Household checklist

- Segregate waste into wet, dry, and sanitary.
- Install low-flow taps and dual-flush systems.
- Harvest rainwater where possible.
- Plant native trees and protect them through summer.

Turning Barriers Into Steps

Many citizens face limits such as fees they cannot afford, distance from training centres, or lack of guidance. Today, there are workarounds. Online classes cut travel costs. Scholarships and loans support deserving students. Public libraries provide study spaces and internet. Mentorship networks match learners with guides. Government portals for jobs, credit, and skilling are open year-round.

Families can plan together. One member studies while another works. Neighbours share transport. The alumni fund one student from their village each year. Small support systems reduce dropouts and keep dreams alive.

A Simple Scorecard For Every Household

Area	One action this month	One action this year
Learning	Finish one online module	Earn one certificate
Civic life	Attend one ward or village meeting	Lead one neighbourhood project
Work	Improve one skill tied to your role	Mentor one junior
Service	Volunteer for two hours	Support one cause monthly
Health	Start a daily walk	Complete preventive checks
Environment	Segregate waste	Install a water or energy saver

India's strength grows when crores of citizens take steps like these. A student who studies with focus. A worker who learns a new tool. A voter who asks questions and then votes with care. A neighbour who helps a senior get to a clinic. These acts do not make headlines. They make a nation.

Each person carries a piece of India's future. Learn. Work with pride. Help someone. Care for water and trees. Speak for what is right. When millions live by these simple rules, progress moves from speeches to streets, and the promise of a developed India turns into daily life.

Educational Institutions: Creating Knowledge Societies

From the hands of citizens, we move to the homes of learning. Every strong nation rests on strong classrooms, labs, libraries, studios, and workshops. Schools shape habits and hope. Colleges and universities shape skill and vision. Research centres turn questions into answers that serve people. When these places work well, a country grows wiser, safer, and more confident.

Quality Education That Lifts Lives

A child who reads with ease and counts with comfort gains a life-long advantage. Schools introduce maths, science, language, arts, and social studies in ways that build curiosity. Good classrooms mix books with doing. Science labs, art rooms, coding clubs, gardens, and sports fields help children learn by practice. Teachers who receive steady training and support bring lessons to life and keep learning on track.

Higher education and vocational training take the baton. Engineers, doctors, nurses, teachers, managers, farmers, and social workers learn in settings that demand both theory and practice. Workshops, internships, rural postings, and capstone projects turn knowledge into solutions. An engineering team working on a small solar pump for a village, a group of medical students running a weekend clinic, a design class building low-cost classroom furniture, all these efforts grow skills and serve people at the same time.

Learning Pathway At A Glance

Stage	Focus	Outcome
School years	Reading, numeracy, curiosity, values	Confident learners
Post-school skill	Hands-on training, industry exposure	Job-ready youth
Higher education	Depth in a field, research methods	Professionals and thinkers
Lifelong learning	Short courses, online modules	Adaptable citizens

Research And Innovation With Purpose

Research moves a nation from dependency to leadership. Universities and institutes study crops, rivers, materials, medicines, data, energy, and space. Their work improves yields, saves water, reduces disease, and opens new industries. When a lab teams up with a factory, a hospital, or a farm, ideas travel faster to the field.

Incubation centres and technology parks on campuses help students and faculty turn prototypes into products. Simple procurement routes for pilot projects give new Indian solutions their first market. Journals, patents, open datasets, and shared facilities make the ecosystem generous and productive.

Skills And Employability For A Changing Economy

Institutions must connect learning to work. Courses that blend classroom and shop floor time produce confident graduates. Strong ties with ITIs, MSME clusters, hospitals, banks, farms, and local authorities keep curricula current. Soft skills matter too. Writing, speaking, teamwork, and basic finance help a young person grow on the job.

Short-term programmes and online certificates give working adults a way to upgrade. A nurse learns new protocols. A mechanic adds EV maintenance. A farmer studies soil health and drip systems. A sales associate learns analytics. This culture of continuous learning keeps families secure as the economy evolves.

Ethics And Social Responsibility

Knowledge without character weakens society. Campuses that teach ethics build professionals who place people first. Business programmes that discuss responsible finance, medical schools that teach consent and confidentiality, engineering courses that examine safety and sustainability, research groups that follow clear integrity norms, all of these create trust. Community service credits, legal aid clinics, and social internships turn values into action.

Civic Engagement And Leadership

Student councils, debate societies, cultural forums, and sports teams teach leadership, fair play, and care for the commons. Voter awareness drives, traffic marshals near schools, waste audits in hostels, water-saving plans in canteens, and energy dashboards in labs make campuses centres of civic action. Graduates who have practised participation carry that habit into neighbourhoods and offices.

Global Competence With Indian Grounding

Exchanges, joint degrees, visiting scholars, and international conferences give students a wider lens. Language learning and cross-cultural projects help them work across borders. At the same time, assignments tied to local challenges keep them rooted. A team that benchmarks global best practices and adapts them to an Indian town or district brings the world home in a useful way.

Closing Gaps, Opening Doors

Challenges remain. Access differs by income and location. Some curricula lag behind industry needs. Teacher training is uneven. Labs and libraries need upgrades. These gaps can be closed with focused effort.

- Digital classrooms and e-libraries reach remote schools.
- Scholarships and hostels support rural and first-generation learners.
- Faculty development programmes renew teaching skills.
- Alumni networks mentor students and fund labs.
- Partnerships with industry and hospitals align courses with real work.

Enablers that raise quality

Enabler	What it does	Who benefits
Teacher development	Updates pedagogy and subject depth	Students in every classroom
Industry links	Internships, apprenticeships, live projects	Graduates and employers
Research funding	Seed new ideas and tools	Labs, start-ups, society
Digital access	Courses, content, and services online	Rural and urban learners

When schools teach well, families gain confidence. When colleges and universities link learning to work and service, districts gain strength. When research solves Indian problems at Indian price points, the economy gains independence. Educational institutions turn the energy of a young nation into skill, judgement, and compassion.

This is how a knowledge society grows, one classroom, one lab, and one campus at a time. And with that base firm under our feet, we can now turn to the next partner in India's progress, the media and information platforms that inform citizens and keep public life honest and alive.

Media: Shaping Perceptions and Awareness

Education builds knowledge. Media builds awareness.

It connects people to ideas, issues, and institutions. It shapes what citizens think about, talk about, and act upon. A strong media gives society its eyes and ears. It informs, questions, and inspires. In a developing country like India, the media has carried stories of change from the remotest village to the largest city. It reminds everyone that information is power, and when people are informed, they participate, decide, and move the country forward.

India's media is among the most diverse in the world. It speaks in dozens of languages, reaches every corner through newspapers, television, radio, and digital platforms, and reflects every shade of public life. It reports on policies, innovations, elections, sports, and culture. More importantly, it plays the twin role of educator and watchdog, helping people understand their rights while ensuring that those in power act responsibly.

Educating the Public

The first responsibility of the media is to inform. It tells citizens what their government is doing, how programs are working, and what opportunities are available. For many in rural and remote areas, news broadcasts, local papers, and community radio are the main sources of information about health drives, farming schemes, and employment programs.

When newspapers explain new education policies in simple words, or when television shows highlight women-led entrepreneurship, it connects policy to people's lives. During health emergencies, such as the COVID-19 pandemic, media platforms became essential in spreading information on safety measures, vaccination, and relief. Stories from local reporters guided relief teams and drew attention to communities in need.

Media also turns learning into an everyday conversation. Documentaries and feature programs break down complex issues, from digital safety and financial planning to environmental protection and public health, so that every citizen can understand and act. A documentary on river conservation can move a community to start a clean-up drive. A podcast on personal finance can encourage families to plan better. This is how information turns into empowerment.

Keeping Power Accountable

A healthy democracy stands on transparency. Media brings this transparency by keeping public institutions open to scrutiny. It asks questions that others hesitate to ask. Investigative reporting exposes corruption, delays, and misuse of public resources. It gives citizens evidence to demand answers.

Stories on pollution, public health lapses, or rural infrastructure gaps have often led to policy corrections. Journalists, editors, and fact-checkers who work with courage and discipline make sure that truth reaches people even when it is inconvenient to those in authority.

Media also prevents small problems from turning into crises. Reporting on school dropouts, rising prices, or failing water systems allows quick response before damage spreads. Citizen journalism on digital platforms has given every person with a phone the power to report and seek attention for issues that need fixing. It is this constant watchfulness that strengthens democracy.

Encouraging Civic Participation

In a large and diverse country, the media acts as a link between citizens and their leaders. It helps people understand how their vote matters, how laws are made, and how budgets affect their daily lives. During elections, responsible coverage helps citizens make informed choices. In local governance, news stories and talk shows encourage participation in panchayat meetings, city councils, and public consultations.

Television debates and editorials often spark dialogue on social issues – women's safety, education, sanitation, or digital rights. Social campaigns on television and radio have played a major role in spreading the message of Swachh Bharat Abhiyan, Beti Bachao Beti Padhao, and Pulse Polio. Through these efforts, media has proven that communication can bring behavioural change at scale.

Social media has added a new dimension to civic engagement. It has made dialogue two-way. Citizens can now share feedback, join causes, and contribute to movements for better governance, environment, or social equality. Whether it is raising funds for a health emergency or calling attention to a civic issue, digital platforms have amplified the citizen's voice.

Driving Innovation and Entrepreneurship

Media gives recognition to those who build and create. By telling the stories of small entrepreneurs, scientists, farmers, and innovators, it encourages others to dream bigger. A feature on a start-up in a small town can attract investors. An article on a farmer using solar pumps can inspire thousands of others to adopt new technology.

Business newspapers and technology magazines highlight developments in artificial intelligence, clean energy, digital finance, and biotechnology, helping readers see the direction of the future economy. When people read about innovation, they start believing that creativity and hard work can change their own circumstances. Media, in this way, spreads a culture of confidence and entrepreneurship.

Many television channels and online platforms now host dedicated programs for young entrepreneurs, showcasing new ideas and connecting innovators to mentors and markets. By spotlighting success stories, the media creates a cycle where progress inspires more progress.

Shaping Values and National Character

Media does more than inform; it shapes how people think and what they value. When reporting is responsible and balanced, it builds trust. When entertainment content highlights empathy, unity, and respect, it strengthens the moral fibre of society.

Television shows and films have the power to change attitudes. They can promote gender equality, environmental care, and respect for diversity. When movies celebrate honesty or sacrifice, they remind people of the values that built the nation. When television covers festivals from every community, it reinforces the message that India's diversity is its strength.

Media also influences how young people see the world. News on innovation, sports, science, and social work gives them role models. When they see people from ordinary backgrounds achieving extraordinary results, they learn that progress is open to all who work with purpose.

Meeting Challenges with Integrity

The influence of the media comes with responsibility. In an age where news travels instantly, misinformation can spread equally fast. False reports and sensationalism can divide people and weaken trust. Commercial pressures and political influence sometimes distort priorities.

Yet, these challenges have also led to stronger systems. Fact-checking teams now verify content before it reaches readers. Independent media houses and journalists continue to uphold ethics, even under pressure. Social media platforms are building tools to flag misleading information. Across the country, citizens are learning media literacy, how to question sources, check facts, and distinguish between opinion and truth.

Ethical journalism will always be the core of progress. Truth-telling, fairness, and accuracy are not ideals; they are necessities for a stable, informed, and confident nation.

Media as a Partner in Development

Media is a force that unites information with action. It spreads awareness about government schemes, tracks how projects are implemented, and celebrates achievements that deserve recognition. It connects distant communities by sharing lessons from one region with another. A success story in rural electrification in Gujarat can inspire action in Assam. A women's cooperative featured on television can motivate others to form similar groups.

When the media highlights positive change, it creates hope. When it investigates wrongdoing, it creates correction. When it educates, it builds understanding. In doing all this, it becomes a silent partner in development.

The strength of India's democracy lies in its ability to think, question, and act together. Media makes this possible. It brings the nation into one conversation, from policymaker to worker, from farmer to scientist.

By keeping truth in focus and people at the centre, the media helps India grow wiser, fairer, and stronger each day.

Farmers and Agricultural Stakeholders

The story of India begins in its soil.

Before industries, highways, and tall buildings, it was farming that sustained life and shaped communities. Even today, farmers remain at the heart of India's strength. Agriculture provides livelihood to millions, feeds families, supports industries, and carries the cultural soul of the country.

India stands among the most agriculturally gifted nations in the world. Its lands are fertile, its climate diverse, and its farming traditions deep and time-tested. From the rich alluvial plains of the Ganga and Brahmaputra to the black soils of the Deccan plateau, from the tea gardens of Assam to the spice farms of Kerala, every region tells a story of abundance. The red soils of Tamil Nadu, the loamy fields of Punjab, and the coastal stretches of Maharashtra and Gujarat all produce crops that reach every corner of the world.

India ranks among the top producers of rice, wheat, pulses, fruits, vegetables, milk, and spices. It grows over 320 million tonnes of food grains each year and is the largest exporter of rice and spices globally. Its farmers cultivate one of the widest ranges of crops on the planet, sustained by over 140 million hectares of arable land. This diversity is both a gift and a responsibility, proving that the nation's prosperity is rooted in the dedication of those who till its soil.

The Core of Development

Agriculture is more than an economic sector. It is the base that supports every other activity. When harvests are strong, markets are vibrant, factories run, and households have stability. Every ton of grain or litre of milk represents far more than a number; it carries the labour, skill, and care of millions.

Farming influences nearly half of India's population. It contributes close to one-fifth of national income and ensures food security for over a billion people. When agriculture grows, rural incomes rise, education improves, and communities thrive.

India's farming heritage has shown resilience across centuries. From the early irrigation systems of the Indus Valley to the Green Revolution that secured self-sufficiency in the 1960s, and now to the digital and sustainable revolutions of today, the farmer has constantly adapted and moved forward.

Modern and Sustainable Practices

Across the country, fields are changing. Farmers are using machinery, data, and modern techniques to produce more from every acre. Tractors and harvesters save time and effort. Soil testing tells farmers what nutrients the land needs. Drip irrigation saves water. Mobile phones carry weather forecasts and market prices to every village.

Technology is no longer distant from the farm. Drones help monitor crop health, while solar pumps replace diesel engines. Young farmers use mobile applications to track rainfall and manage sowing. These innovations increase yield, reduce waste, and bring efficiency to every stage of farming.

Sustainability is now becoming part of this new movement. Organic manure, mixed cropping, and rotation preserve soil health. Watershed projects recharge groundwater. Natural farming reduces chemical use and keeps the food system healthy. These practices balance production with care for the earth. Farmers are proving that growth and sustainability can go hand in hand.

Cooperatives and Farmer Organisations

One of India's greatest agricultural strengths lies in collective action. Cooperatives and Farmer Producer Organisations (FPOs) have given small farmers a shared voice and stronger market power. Dairy cooperatives like Amul transformed rural Gujarat into a hub of prosperity. Farmer cooperatives in Maharashtra and Karnataka did the same for sugar and cotton.

These organisations connect farmers to credit, technology, and markets. They reduce dependence on middlemen and ensure that profits reach those who do the work. They also bring education and training, helping farmers learn modern techniques, handle finances, and understand trade.

When farmers work together, they gain bargaining strength, shared infrastructure, and collective pride. This spirit of cooperation turns agriculture from survival into enterprise.

Digital Growth and Market Access

Digital technology has changed how farming connects with the economy. Platforms such as the National Agriculture Market (eNAM) allow farmers to sell produce across states. Market prices are now available instantly on mobile phones. Digital payments bring transparency and faster transactions.

Startups are building tools that make farming smarter. Soil sensors, satellite-based mapping, and digital advisory services help farmers make better choices. Supply chain solutions reduce delays, while logistics platforms link farms to supermarkets and exporters. These changes make agriculture more connected and more rewarding.

Technology also brings fairness. With data and connectivity, farmers can reach buyers directly, negotiate better prices, and plan storage and distribution without being dependent on intermediaries. The farm is now part of a digital ecosystem that supports both smallholders and large producers alike.

Farmers as Guardians of the Environment

Every farmer is also a steward of the environment. Fields and forests, rivers and rainfall, all are bound together. Sustainable practices like water harvesting, solar-powered irrigation, organic fertilisers, and tree planting help protect these natural resources.

Programs such as PM-KUSUM promote solar energy on farms, reducing costs and pollution. Agroforestry creates income while restoring green cover. When farmers manage land with care, they preserve biodiversity, recharge groundwater, and reduce emissions. Their actions keep India's ecological balance intact while ensuring long-term productivity.

Challenges That Need Attention

Agriculture faces real challenges that must be addressed with urgency and empathy. Small landholdings limit scale. Access to credit and insurance is uneven. Post-harvest losses remain high due to inadequate storage. Markets fluctuate, and climate change brings unpredictable weather.

These issues demand solutions that combine technology with policy. Affordable loans, reliable irrigation, cold chain infrastructure, and transparent market systems are essential. Strengthening training and rural education will help farmers use modern tools and understand new markets.

Government schemes like PM-KISAN, soil health cards, and the Agriculture Infrastructure Fund are important steps, but their success depends on how effectively they reach every farmer. Rural prosperity grows when information, finance, and opportunity flow freely to those who work the land.

Opportunities for a New Era

Agriculture today is filled with promise. India is seeing rapid growth in horticulture, floriculture, dairy, and fisheries. Organic products are finding buyers both at home and abroad. Food processing industries are adding value and creating employment. The future lies in diversification, moving from subsistence to high-value crops and from raw produce to finished goods.

Collaboration is the key. Farmers, research institutions, private companies, and the government are working together to make farming smarter and more sustainable. Research on high-yield seeds, water-saving techniques, and pest-resistant crops continues to improve resilience. Rural entrepreneurship is turning young farmers into agri-business leaders who see the land not as a burden but as an opportunity.

Farmers as Nation Builders

Every grain in the granary carries a farmer's faith and effort. Every meal on the table begins in a field where someone woke before dawn and worked until sunset. The story of India's farmers is one of quiet strength and enduring hope. They sustain the economy, feed millions, and guard the land that gives life to all.

When farmers prosper, the entire country moves forward. A strong and secure agricultural base builds resilience against crisis, ensures food security, and fuels growth across sectors. Supporting farmers through education, technology, and fair policy is an investment in national pride and stability.

The soil of India holds more than crops; *it holds history, heritage, and human potential.*

International Stakeholders: Global Partnerships

From the village well to the factory gate, India's progress is built at home. Yet every step is stronger when the world walks with us. Partners abroad bring capital, technology, new ideas, and open doors to markets. In return, India offers talent, scale, and solutions that work at population size. This exchange makes our journey faster and steadier.

Foreign Investment That Builds And Employs

When investments come into ports, metros, industrial parks, hospitals, data centres, and clean energy, they do more than add money. They bring know-how, quality systems, and new jobs. Global auto makers setting up plants have seeded entire supplier ecosystems in Pune, Chennai, Sanand, and Manesar. Electronics assembly linked to international brands has lifted clusters in Noida and Sriperumbudur. Wind and solar developers from across the world have helped build large parks in Rajasthan, Gujarat, and Tamil Nadu, cutting power costs and raising green capacity.

With these projects come modern production methods, safety standards, and management practices. Indian teams trained in these systems carry the learning to local vendors and future ventures. The result is higher productivity, better products, and stronger export potential.

Technology And Research, Shared And Scaled

Partnerships with universities, labs, and companies overseas help India solve hard problems faster. Joint work in vaccines and diagnostics strengthened our health response. Collaboration in crop science, remote sensing, and water management has raised yields and saved resources. In information technology and artificial intelligence, Indian engineers work with global teams on secure payments, language tools, and logistics engines that serve millions.

When research travels both ways, everyone advances. Indian institutes gain access to advanced equipment and methods. Partners gain the benefits of India's talent, datasets, and use cases. Start-ups born in campus incubators often grow through cross-border grants, mentorship, and pilot customers abroad.

Trade That Turns Strength Into Opportunity

Selling to the world creates income and discipline. Software and business services, pharmaceuticals, textiles, auto components, chemicals, and agricultural products now reach customers in more than a hundred countries. Meeting global standards raises quality at home. Competing abroad pushes firms to improve design, packaging, delivery time, and after-sales support. Importing key equipment and inputs, while building more at home, helps industry climb the value chain.

Trade agreements and participation in bodies such as the World Trade Organization provide rules and forums to resolve differences. They also open routes for cooperation in customs modernisation, standards, and digital trade.

Support That Multiplies Public Good

International financial institutions and partner countries often co-fund projects that change daily life. Rural roads, metro lines, clean water systems, waste treatment plants, and power grids grow faster when concessional finance and technical assistance are available. Programmes in teacher training, public health, disaster management, and urban planning benefit from tested templates and neutral evaluations.

Capacity building is as valuable as money. Workshops for officials, twinning arrangements between cities, and sector-specific task forces help Indian teams avoid common pitfalls and adopt what works.

Joint Action For Climate And Sustainability

The climate challenge respects no border. India's commitments under global agreements are backed by partnerships in solar, wind, storage, green hydrogen, electric mobility, and energy efficiency. Technology sharing and blended finance help projects reach commercial scale sooner. Programmes in river rejuvenation, coastal protection, and forestry gain from global science and community practices tested elsewhere.

This cooperation supports a development path where growth, jobs, and clean air move together. It also creates new industries, from battery materials to recycling and repair services.

Learning Across Borders

Conferences, fellowships, and exchange programmes expand horizons. Engineers, doctors, teachers, administrators, and entrepreneurs who train abroad bring back tools, case studies, and contacts. Joint ventures expose Indian firms to global procurement, compliance, and customer expectations. In turn, Indian approaches to digital public goods, low-cost health solutions, and large-scale service delivery are now shaping programmes in Asia, Africa, and Latin America.

Working Through Risks With A Steady Hand

Partnerships come with choices. Over-reliance on a single source of capital, technology, or market can create strain if conditions change. Differences in rules and intellectual property regimes need careful handling. The answer is balance. Build strong domestic research and manufacturing, diversify partners, encourage joint development rather than only purchase, and keep data and security safeguards tight. This way, international ties strengthen resilience rather than weaken it.

India As A Giver And A Guide

India is a partner, not a bystander. Peacekeeping missions, humanitarian aid, vaccine supplies, digital platforms shared as public goods, and training for officials from other countries show a spirit of cooperation. As our economy expands, so does our ability to invest abroad, to co-create technologies, and to help set fair rules for the future of trade, tech, and climate action.

Serve before speaking. Share credit. Fix leaks before launching new schemes. Spend on maintenance as seriously as on new assets. Tell the truth with numbers and stories. Keep promises small enough to meet and large enough to matter.

A nation of this size advances when crores of daily actions line up. A teacher who lifts a class, a nurse who keeps a clinic open, a driver who keeps a bus on time, a coder who secures a system, a farmer who saves water, a judge who closes a case, a councillor who fixes a drain, a founder who pays on time, a reporter who informs with care. This is how plans become a public good.

We have the people, the ideas, the tools, and the will. The work now is to turn every promise into proof, in every district and every lane, so that a developed India is experienced in homes, not only read in reports.

✦ ✦ ✦

5

CHANGE

"Arise, awake, and stop not till the goal is reached."

– Swami Vivekananda

Change through Innovation and Entrepreneurship: The Heart of India's Movement

Entrepreneurs: Catalysts for jobs, economy, and impact

Entrepreneurs do more than open companies; they turn ideas into livelihoods, link talent to purpose, and convert local problems into national solutions. In a country of 140 crore people, every enterprise becomes a training ground, a supplier network, and a signal of confidence for an entire community. The goal before us is clear. Enterprise must aim at meaningful innovation, serve real needs, and scale with integrity so growth lifts people as well as numbers.

Evidence of this possibility already lives in our recent past. Firms such as Infosys and TCS began as small teams with precise discipline, then grew into institutions that employ lakhs, shape global delivery standards, and seed entire ecosystems of institutes, testing labs, and vendor clusters. Their rise did more than raise revenue; it set habits around quality, mentorship, and steady investment in people. That culture of seriousness is a national asset.

A similar pattern flows through digital finance. Platforms like Paytm and Razorpay made payments simple for the street vendor and the small clinic, for the tuition teacher and the home entrepreneur. When a neighbourhood merchant accepts a scan-and-pay transaction and settles accounts without delay, formality grows, credit histories form, and the young founder can bill on day one without a long queue at a counter. UPI strengthened this shift with instant, low-friction transfers between bank accounts, turning the mobile phone into a dependable business tool for every district.

India's base of micro, small, and medium enterprises anchors this movement. These firms contribute a significant share of GDP and exports, absorb young workers, and stitch villages to city supply chains. When a small unit meets a delivery date, pays on time, and certifies quality, trust compounds across the chain. That trust is developed in practice. It reduces the cost of doing business, invites fair credit, and draws new learners into the workforce.

Entrepreneurship also carries a social and environmental charge. Founders who design for clean water, soil health, efficient energy, and last-mile access prove that profit and responsibility can move together. A solar service in a hamlet that lights homes and powers a sewing machine, a telemedicine kiosk that shortens travel for a routine consultation, a cold-chain solution that saves a farmer's produce during peak heat, each of these changes the daily math of a family. When thousands of such efforts run with care, the national picture shifts without slogans.

The next wave will rise where need and know-how meet. Digital public infrastructure lowers barriers for identity, payments, and secure consent, which allows young teams to build trustworthy products for millions at low cost. Affordable software for accounting and inventory can lift productivity in workshops and kirana stores. Precision tools in agriculture can limit waste and raise incomes. Clean energy services can trim bills for households and factories while meeting climate goals. Health and learning solutions can reach smaller cities with dignity and speed.

Policy and institutions have a role that is both simple and decisive. Keep the cost of trust low through paperless verification and e-signature. Clear invoices on time in public procurement, so small firms hire and invest. Link research labs with industrial clusters and set challenge grants that reward tested outcomes. Publish service-level timelines for approvals so a founder spends more hours with customers than with files. When the rules are clear and time is honoured, ambition flowers in every tier.

Founders, in turn, can own a compact that makes growth steady. Build for unit economics from the first customer. Keep books clean and taxes current. Train first-time workers and promote from within. Choose markets where value repeats and deepens over time. Share playbooks with peers so common mistakes fade and common standards rise. This conduct turns a promising company into an institution and an institution into a national example.

Innovation is a daily habit, not a festival. It is the decision to improve one product, serve one more customer, teach one colleague a new skill, and keep every promise made yesterday. India has the tools in hand: a digital stack the world studies, an enterprise base that already exports to distant markets, and a young workforce ready to learn. If we build with care, compete with courage, and keep the gains inclusive, entrepreneurship will become more than commerce. It will become pride made visible in the lives we improve.

Solving Real Indian Problems

India's size, diversity, and youthful energy make it a place where real problems meet real ingenuity. Entrepreneurs who choose hard problems, healthcare access, clean energy for villages, reliable logistics for farmers, and skills for first-time workers do more than build companies. They lift incomes, open markets, and set new standards for service. The canvas is huge. The need is clear. When solutions are rooted in local realities and built to scale, impact follows.

Araku Coffee: Empowering Farmers, Building a Brand

High in the Eastern Ghats, smallholder Adivasi families turned a fragile livelihood into a premium brand. With long-term support from the Naandi Foundation, farmers adopted organic methods, improved post-harvest quality, and connected directly to global buyers. In 2017, the ARAKU brand opened a flagship café in Paris, a signal that Indian origin coffee could command quality premiums when traceability, training, and market access came together. The model married fair pricing, soil health, and consistent quality, and it unlocked pride as well as profit.

India has millions of small farms. When one cluster shows how aggregation, quality control, and transparent contracts work, others can copy and adapt. The lesson is simple: organise producers, invest in skills, keep value in the community, and tell an authentic product story.

Practo: Access to Care, From Phone to Clinic

Healthcare in India is dense in cities and thin in many districts. Practo built a single front door for patients: search for verified doctors, book appointments, store digital records, consult online, and navigate insurance and hospital workflows. On the supply side, hospitals and clinics use their software for scheduling, billing, and analytics. The result is shorter wait times, clearer records, and fewer missed follow-ups.

This digital front door sits alongside a public telemedicine backbone that shows how large India's demand for remote care really is. The government's eSanjeevani platform has crossed tens of crores of consultations, proving that virtual care can be safe, fast, and affordable at a national scale. Entrepreneurs can plug into this momentum with diagnostics at the doorstep, e-pharmacy last-mile delivery, and AI triage tools tuned to Indian languages.

Four Arenas Where Founders Move the Needle

1) **Rural healthcare.** Telemedicine works when it is paired with nurse-led kiosks, low-cost diagnostics, and reliable referrals. Use simple interfaces, local

language support, and outcome tracking. Tie into public rails like eSanjeevani for reach, then layer private services for speed and choice.

2) **Urban mobility.** Electric two-wheelers are cutting commute costs and emissions. India sold roughly 1.2 million electric scooters in the year to March 2025, yet penetration is still in single digits, which means there is room to grow with better charging, smarter batteries, and service networks that reach dense neighbourhoods. Founders can build for delivery fleets, financing, and battery health scoring.

3) **Education and skills.** Young workers need stackable skills they can earn while they learn. Edtech that tracks competency, partners with local employers, and proves placement will win trust. Practice labs for trades, cloud labs for software, and peer mentors for soft skills help first-generation learners cross the gap from coursework to a steady job.

4) **Sustainable energy.** Village microgrids and rooftop solar give households and shops dependable power for lights, pumps, and point-of-sale devices. Lenders and operators are already scaling mini-grids with prepaid meters and remote monitoring. Link this with the cold-chain for farm produce, and the value of each unit of power multiplies.

What Makes an "India-fit" Solution

- **Design for constraints.** Patchy bandwidth, heat, dust, and cash-flow variability are design inputs, not afterthoughts.

- **Trust through transparency.** Clear pricing, service levels, and grievance redressal build adoption faster than discounts.
- **Public rails, private innovation.** Identity, payments, logistics, and health exchanges are shared rails; founders build specialised services on top.
- **Regional first, national next.** Solve deeply in one state, localise language and workflows, then expand.

The Payoff

When entrepreneurs solve India-specific problems, three things rise together: incomes, inclusion, and confidence. Farmers become brand owners. Patients become informed decision-makers. Students become earners. Clean power turns long evenings into productive hours. Each venture is a job creator, a skill engine, and a proof point that growth can be both profitable and fair.

This is how a nation of many languages and many dreams moves as one, through solutions that respect people's time, strengthen local systems, and scale with integrity. Build for India, and you build for a world that looks more like India every year.

Innovation with Purpose

Innovation matters when it moves a life forward, lowers a bill, saves an hour, or catches a disease early. India has enough talent to build brilliant things; the real test is whether those ideas serve people where they live. Purpose turns skill into nation-building.

What purposeful innovation looks like

Health that reaches the last mile: Niramai Health Analytics built Thermalytix, a screening tool that uses thermal imaging to help detect breast abnormalities without radiation or painful compression. Peer-reviewed studies on Thermalytix report high sensitivity with promising specificity, pointing to a low-cost pathway for large-scale screening in busy public systems. When a test is non-invasive and portable, a primary health centre can screen more women, earlier, with less fear and fewer barriers.

India has scaled the telemedicine rails that such diagnostics can ride. The government's eSanjeevani platform has logged crores of consultations, relieving pressure on hospitals and taking specialist advice into smaller towns. State rollouts show steady month-on-month use, with lakhs of virtual visits supported by thousands of doctors across thousands of centres. Purpose and platform together place care closer to the citizen.

Clean power that creates jobs and cuts import risk: ReNew is among India's largest renewable energy companies, operating utility-scale solar and wind projects that feed the grid at scale. Its portfolio runs into tens of gigawatts of installed and committed capacity, part of a national shift that has pushed India's total non-fossil capacity toward the 200-plus GW mark. Each new megawatt brings construction work today and maintenance jobs tomorrow, while lowering the fuel bill India pays the world.

Learning that adapts to the learner: India's EdTech pioneers showed that adaptive content and vernacular delivery can keep a child engaged in a crowded home.

The strongest use cases are not screens replacing schools, but tools that support teachers, track progress, and widen access to high-quality practice material for entrance tests and skills. Where districts pair devices with coaching and guardrails, completion rates rise, and parents see value in each hour spent.

Energy access that lifts incomes: SELCO India proved that solar is not only an engineering story but also a service model. By tailoring systems to street vendors, small clinics, and home enterprises, and by aligning repayments with daily cash flows, SELCO turned kilowatt hours into earnings and study hours. The lesson is clear: design the finance with the same care as the hardware, and clean energy becomes a livelihood tool.

Why India can scale purposeful innovation

- **Digital public rails:** The India Stack, Aadhaar, UPI, and consent frameworks let startups authenticate users, move money instantly, and earn trust. UPI alone processes billions of payments each month, a level that enables micro-subscriptions, village-level commerce, and instant refunds for government schemes.
- **Falling costs in renewables:** Utility-scale solar tariffs have stayed competitive with coal in many auctions, which helps states lock in long-term power at stable prices while meeting climate targets.
- **A huge user base online:** Hundreds of millions use mobile data at low cost, which gives health,

skilling, and farm apps a real shot at scale when they solve a daily pain point.

Building for impact, not headlines

1. **Start with the problem, then choose the tech:** Niramai began with the screening gap and picked thermal imaging because it fits Indian clinics. That order matters.
2. **Design for public systems:** If a tool works inside a PHC or a government school, scale follows through state adoption. eSanjeevani shows how.
3. **Match economics to reality:** Solar for micro-businesses only sticks when payment schedules mirror cash flows. SELCO's field model is the template.
4. **Prove, then partner:** ReNew's utility projects grew through bankable pilots and long-term offtake. Deep partnerships beat one-off installs.

The north star

Innovation with purpose is simple to recognise. A mother saves a day's travel because a doctor visits her screen at noon. A student in a small town finishes a practice set that finally makes calculus click. A weaver pays less for power and keeps more from each sale. A nurse uses a new tool that catches a tumour early. Each of these is progress that compounds.

India's promise is not a theory. The infrastructure is here, the builders are here, the users are ready. When we align invention with need, price with ability to pay, and data with dignity, we do more than create companies. We build confidence, village by village and city by city, that the future can be fairer and faster at the same time.

Scaling Globally to Amplify Impact

India teaches founders to work with noise, price sensitivity, patchy infrastructure, and millions of users who decide within seconds whether a product earns a place on their home screen. If something stands up to that test, it can travel. The path is simple in spirit: build for India first, then carry the strongest playbooks to new regions, and grow with care.

Start with why this approach works. Serving large, diverse cohorts at home forces discipline in cost, onboarding, support, and fraud control. Teams learn to watch unit economics daily and ship only what the customer will pay for. That rhythm builds muscle. It also makes pricing honest when the product steps into Southeast Asia, the Gulf, Africa, or select Western cities, where small and medium businesses look for reliable tools at fair terms.

Consider what global movement has looked like in practice. Zomato began with listings and reviews, added delivery and ads, and learned which markets reward depth over spread. The company kept its strongest positions and trimmed where partner density or local rules did not fit the model. OYO pushed tech-led standardisation for small hotels, upgraded thousands of rooms, then focused on regions where supply owners and guests stayed loyal to the platform. Neither story is a straight line. The lesson is to expand with a clear cash plan, adjust when the ground shifts, and keep the home market as the anchor.

Software made in India sells well abroad because the sales motion is lightweight and the product does not pretend to be something it is not. A two-person inside-sales team in Chennai or Bengaluru can close pilots in Dubai, Nairobi, or Warsaw if the tool saves time and shows clear payback. Support runs long hours from India, documentation is clean, and releases land on schedule. Over time, this becomes an export engine with healthy margins and compounding references.

Fintech shows another way to carry ideas outward. The rails built at home, for instance, low-cost payments and digital identity prove that inclusion and scale can sit together. When these designs inform cross-border pilots or bilateral links, India exports more than code. It exports a way of thinking about public digital goods, merchant economics, and consumer trust.

For founders planning the next step, a few habits help:

- Choose markets by adjacency, not hype: Look for places where smartphone use, price points, and small-business structures feel familiar.
- Keep core tech and security in India, hire local sales and compliance early, and respect the regulator's calendar as much as the customer's calendar.
- Price with intent: Transparent tiers beat deep discounts that hide a weak fit.
- Win with partners: Telcos, banks, and distributors can shrink acquisition costs and build trust faster than a cold outreach list.

Global growth should serve a national purpose as well. Foreign revenue stabilises cash flows, brings in capital, and funds the next wave of Indian founders.

Each product that lands overseas becomes a quiet ambassador for Indian engineering and customer care. When a city far from home runs on Indian payroll software or a hotel group upgrades through an Indian stack, it shapes how people see the country. That is soft power with a ledger.

Keep the tone of this journey grounded. Expansion is a choice, not a race. Some products deserve depth at home before any move abroad. Others earn the right to step out quickly because the need is universal. The test is simple: does the product solve a real pain, at a price the market accepts, with support the team can sustain for years.

India first, then the world, is a working sequence. It begins with adoption in towns and metros, continues with proof in nearby regions, and matures with selective presence in large economies. Founders who move with patience, clean books, and respect for local rules do more than grow their companies. They widen India's circle of trust in technology and design.

Great aim belongs here. Build where the signals are clear, carry the craft with care, and let the results speak in new languages.

Entrepreneurs as Mentors: Multiplying Impact

Mentorship is where experience turns into a public good. A founder who has lived through product missteps, cash crunches, and the grind of hiring can save a young team months of trial and error. That saving compounds. One hour of clear advice today becomes better pricing next week, tighter unit economics next quarter, and stronger jobs a year later.

India already has the scaffolding for this kind of transfer. Indian Angel Network pairs first-time founders with seasoned operators across finance, go-to-market, and governance. NASSCOM's 10,000 Startups program matches teams with domain coaches, connects them to pilots, and pushes them to refine compliance and security standards that global customers expect. TiE chapters in Delhi, Bengaluru, Hyderabad, and Chennai run mentor circles where founders receive blunt feedback on customer acquisition, cash flow discipline, and hiring plans. These forums lower the odds of common mistakes and raise the floor on quality.

The effect shows up in numbers that matter. Startups with structured mentors tend to survive their first two years at higher rates than those without guidance. They close pilots faster because a mentor can make the first five calls. They waste less on features no one needs because someone at the table asks for proof before code. In practical terms, this means more stable salaries, cleaner books, and customers who stay.

The circle is widening. State platforms such as T-Hub in Hyderabad, Kerala Startup Mission in Thiruvananthapuram, and StartupTN in Chennai pair founders with industry leaders and investors. IIT and IIM incubators now track mentor hours as seriously as funds raised, and many tie the next tranche of support to proof from mentor-led milestones. Corporate programs run by banks, telecom firms, and manufacturers bring mentors from procurement, cybersecurity, and regulatory teams into the room so a startup learns how to pass vendor diligence before the first enterprise pitch.

Two patterns repeat wherever this works well.

First, mentors are specific: They do not give speeches. They review a pricing sheet, rewrite a sales email, and rehearse a demo until the timing lands. A product leader will sit with the team and set a release calendar that can actually be met. A finance mentor will walk through the gross margin line by line and flag what must improve before any scale.

Second, the help is local and real-time: India's markets are diverse in income, languages, and rules. A mentor in Coimbatore can warn a hardware startup about service expectations in tier-2 cities. A mentor in Ahmedabad can explain why a distributor will ask for credit terms and how to protect cash. This kind of advice fits the ground.

The platforms are growing in depth as well as reach. Rainmatter, seeded by Zerodha, combines capital with hands-on guidance in fintech and climate. Founders share recruiting playbooks, compliance checklists, and vendor references. Women-led cohorts through organisations such as WE Hub in Telangana and private funds run focused sessions on cap tables, leadership, and market entry, so more women scale companies with confidence and control.

Schools and campuses are joining in. Mentor programs at IITs, IISc, and ISB bring alumni back to guide labs on licensing, patents, and global partnerships. Many colleges now run semester-long clinics where mentors and students build working pilots for local hospitals, municipal bodies, and small manufacturers. These pilots turn into paying customers, and students graduate with a track record rather than a pitch deck alone.

The public stack strengthens all of this. With UPI, GST, and e-invoicing in place, mentors can ask a founder to bring real dashboards to the meeting. Margins, returns, defaults, and cohort stickiness show up in numbers instead of anecdotes. Progress becomes visible, and arguments become smaller.

What should founders do to make the most of this network?

- Set clear asks before every session: One metric, one decision, one document to improve.
- Share the full picture: Mentors cannot fix what they cannot see.
- Track outcomes from each conversation: Close a pilot, change a price, or cut a feature.
- Give back early: Run a monthly clinic for college teams or review resumes for a smaller startup. Teaching sharpens your own craft.

What should mentors hold themselves to?

- Keep time and keep promises: Send the intro you offered. Return with the template you mentioned.
- Stay current. Markets move: Read the latest rules, pricing trends, and security standards before advising.
- Guard integrity, steer clear of conflicts: Set boundaries on compensation. Put the founder's interest first.

When this culture takes root, the impact multiplies beyond any single company. Better survival rates mean steadier employment. Cleaner processes lift vendor networks and local services. Stronger exports improve the balance sheet of the country. A founder who has been guided well will mentor others. That is how an ecosystem becomes a movement.

India's strength is scale, skill, and a habit of learning in public. Mentorship turns those strengths into momentum. One lamp lights another. Then a street. Then a city. Then the map.

Entrepreneurship for National Safety and Security

Security is work you can touch. A soldier needs eyes in the sky, ears on the ground, and tools that do their job in heat, dust, and rain. When founders build those tools at home, the country gains strength, saves foreign exchange, and creates careers that last.

India is already moving. Defence production has crossed the lakh-crore mark in recent years, and defence exports are climbing year on year. Policy has cleared space for builders through higher automatic FDI limits, faster procurement tracks, and Positive Indigenisation Lists that tell the market which parts and systems will be sourced locally. That mix of demand, finance, and clarity is turning small labs and workshops into suppliers for real missions.

Startups have stepped forward. ideaForge turned a student project into UAV fleets that patrol borders, map disaster zones, and support units in tough terrain. Big Bang Boom Solutions won a large order for counter-drone systems that guard bases and convoys. NewSpace Research & Technologies is working on swarming and teaming so that many small drones can carry out complex tasks together. Tonbo Imaging builds electro-optic sights and fire-control brains that help personnel see clearly at night and through haze. Sagar Defence Engineering has shown long-range autonomous surface vessels that can watch coasts and move supplies without a crew. These are Indian designs, Indian teams, and Indian test ranges. The learning stays here, the jobs stay here.

Why this push matters:

- **Readiness**: Local design allows quick upgrades when field units send feedback. A change in software, a stronger motor, a sturdier gimbal, all can ship in weeks, not months.
- **Reliability**: Spares and service sit closer to the user. Turnaround shrinks. Equipment returns to duty faster.
- **Reach**: Dual-use markets keep factories running between defence orders. Surveying farms, inspecting pipelines, scanning mines, and guarding ports, the same core tech earns through civil work.
- **Respect**: Each export builds trust with partners who want dependable kit at sane prices.

What founders can build next:

- **Counter-UAS layers** that blend radars, RF sensors, optics, and AI fusion, plus soft-kill and hard-kill options for cities, bases, and energy corridors.
- **Hardened networks** with post-quantum-ready encryption, secure radios, and routers for tactical use.

- **Space-enabled security** through small satellites for maritime domain awareness, AIS augmentation, and rapid refresh imaging.
- **Materials and propulsion** for lighter armour, high-temperature ceramics, efficient engines for loitering munitions and ISR drones.
- **Safe autonomy** with robust test harnesses, clear rules of engagement baked into code, and on-edge mission retasking.

How to move from demo to deployment:

1. **Co-develop with the user** a Trial on real borders, coasts, deserts, and forests. Field hours beat slide decks.
2. **Design for certification** from day one. Map SQRs, EMI/EMC, environmental tests, air or sea worthiness. Reliability saves lives and time.
3. **Build for the sustainment** of modular parts, line-replaceable units, long-life batteries, and clean manuals in Indian languages.
4. **Protect IP and plan exports.** File, document, and comply with export rules so deals travel well.
5. **Price for the full life cycle.** Upfront cost matters, but the country wins when spares, training, and upgrades are clear and fair.

What government and large buyers can do:

- **Post clear problem statements:** Timelines and budgets, so young firms know where to aim.
- **Expand iDEX-style challenges**: Across the Army, Navy, Air Force, Coast Guard, CAPFs, and key PSUs.

- **Fund test ranges and shared labs**: RF, optics, propulsion, and environmental testing, so small teams can meet standards.
- **Speed up limited-series production**: Bridge the gap between trials and full induction.
- **Pay on time**: Cash flow keeps engineers employed and factories alive.

What investors can do:

- **Back patient hardware**: Drones, optics, radios, motors, and materials need time, but the moat is real.
- **Support dual-use plays**: Sell to both public and private buyers.
- **Add operators as advisors**: Veterans and test pilots shorten cycles and raise product truth.

What universities can do:

- **Run defence design studios** with capstone projects tied to live needs.
- **Open maker floors late** so teams can build after class.
- **Host joint labs** with DPSUs and private primes, with IP pathways that reward students.

The outcomes are practical and human. A drone that endures desert wind can also find flood victims. A coastal vessel that sails through a night squall can also deliver supplies to an island clinic. A secure radio that holds a link under jamming can also keep power crews coordinated during a cyclone. Security work blends into service.

This is an enterprise with a flag in its heart. Meet time and spec. Ship what you promise. Return after-sales calls. Train the unit that will carry your kit into a hard place. Keep improving after version one. Do this again and again, and the result is larger than any single contract. The country stands taller. People find work with purpose. Knowledge compounds in our own soil.

India has the talent, the policy tailwind, and the market. Founders can turn that mix into tools that protect lives and earn respect. Build here, test here, ship from here. When the next patrol lifts off or the next watch begins on a dark shoreline, let the gear in that mission carry the imprint of Indian minds and Indian hands.

Key Areas for Impact-Focused Entrepreneurship

India's energy is real and near at hand. When founders choose problems that touch daily life, growth and dignity move together. Below are the arenas where a builder's effort can shift outcomes at scale, with current signals that show the ground is ready.

Healthcare and Life Sciences

Affordable care at speed changes life chances for millions.

- **Primary care, telemedicine and diagnostics:** Public teleconsultation has crossed the "many tens of millions" mark; eSanjeevani's cumulative consultations are in the multi-crore range, proving that remote care can work outside metros when designed well.

- **Insurance rails:** Ayushman Bharat and state schemes now cover hundreds of millions of low-income citizens, creating demand for low-cost devices, AI triage, e-pharmacy fulfilment, and hospital workflow tools.
- **Where founders can act:** AI-assisted screening for cancer, TB and diabetes; point-of-care devices built for heat, dust and voltage fluctuation; last-mile cold chain with IoT; vernacular symptom checkers; hospital revenue-cycle automation for tier-2 and tier-3 cities.

Education and Skill Development

A young country needs employable skills, not seat counts.

- **Digital public goods already lower the cost to learn:** Platforms such as DIKSHA and SWAYAM reached learners at a national scale during and after the pandemic; Skill India and PMKVY have trained tens of millions since launch, and fresh cohorts keep entering the system each year.
- **Where founders can act:** outcome-priced skilling tied to job guarantees; micro-credentials for shop-floor automation, EV maintenance and heat-resilient construction; AI tutors for state board curricula in Indian languages; school ERP that actually reduces teacher paperwork.

Sustainable Agriculture and Allied Value Chains

Farm income rises when input risk falls and markets open.

- **Irrigation and inputs:** Micro-irrigation under national programs has added millions of hectares over the past decade; water-smart agronomy is now a necessity, not a luxury.
- **Collectives and credit:** Farmer-Producer Organisations (FPOs) and KCC-linked credit create a base for input financing, soil services, and offtake contracts.
- **Where founders can act:** soil testing at panchayat scale; weather-indexed advisory in local languages; traceability for high-margin crops; low-waste cold chains; BNPL for seeds and drip kits tied to harvest payments.

Energy and Environment

Clean power is a growth story and a jobs story.

- **Capacity is rising fast:** India's renewable capacity has reached the hundreds of gigawatts when you include solar, wind and hydro, with MNRE reporting steady year-on-year additions and a long runway ahead.
- **Where founders can act:** rooftop solar for MSMEs with analytics-driven pay-as-you-save; community biogas for wet-waste cities; BESS deployment toolkits for utilities; green-hydrogen balance-of-plant components; precision maintenance for wind fleets.

Urban Infrastructure: Water, Waste, Mobility

Cities will decide productivity for a generation.

- **Solid waste and sanitation:** Under Swachh Bharat Mission-Urban, more cities are processing waste and expanding door-to-door collection; municipal demand exists for tech that proves outcomes.
- **Where founders can act:** SaaS for ward-level waste routing; leak detection for piped water; modular sewage treatment for small towns; EV logistics for hospital supplies and groceries; heat-resilient building materials certified for Indian conditions.

Digital and FinTech

Open rails make inclusion a business model, not a CSR line.

- **UPI keeps compounding:** India's instant payment system processes billions of transactions each month and continues to expand into credit, recurring payments and cross-border corridors.
- **Where founders can act:** fraud-risk engines for small merchants; sachet insurance attached to real transactions; MSME cash-flow lending from GST/UPI exhaust; vernacular wealth platforms for first-time investors; cybersecurity for co-ops and RRBs.

Defence and Security

Indigenisation creates room for deep tech, and the market is growing.

- **Production and exports are up:** Recent years saw record defence production and a rise in exports, with policy pull for domestic design and manufacture.
- **Where founders can act:** dual-use drones and swarms; edge AI for surveillance; secure radios and mesh networks; cyber ranges and red-team services; lightweight composites and power electronics for harsh terrain.

Social Welfare, Women's Enterprise and Rural Development

When women's groups gain capital and markets, the whole village moves.

- **Organised community power:** DAY-NRLM reports millions of self-help groups with pooled savings and growing credit access; these groups are dependable customers and strong distribution partners for essentials and income-generating kits.
- **Where founders can act:** livelihood kits for SHGs in food processing and textiles; tele-law and grievance tools; rural e-commerce with fair returns; climate-risk services for vulnerable districts.

How founders can turn intent into outcomes

1. **Pick a measured gap:** Anchor the product to one public metric that already exists: teleconsultation volume in a district hospital, litres of non-revenue water, feeder losses, SHG loan repayment, and classroom attendance that matches DIKSHA activity.

2. **Build for conditions, not for labs:** Heat, dust, voltage fluctuation, patchy bandwidth and multilingual use are design constraints, not edge cases.
3. **Stand on public rails:** UPI, Aadhaar, ONDC, Account Aggregator, DigiLocker and government APIs reduce friction and CAC when used responsibly.
4. **Price for Indian unit economics:** Small tickets with clear payback beat premium features that need subsidy.
5. **Prove outcomes early:** A block, a ward, or one district with third-party verification is more persuasive than a national press release.
6. **Hire for trust:** Local partnerships with SHG federations, FPOs, panchayats, and district hospitals shorten the learning curve.
7. **Stay transparent on data and safety:** Consent, audit trails and grievance redressal are not paperwork; they are market access.

India's scale rewards those who solve real problems and stay close to the user. The figures above point to markets that are already moving. The work now is to ship, learn, and keep improving until the solution holds under field conditions.

Entrepreneurial Mindset for Impact

"Purpose-driven" is not a label on a pitch deck. It is a way of working that holds up in the field, in the market, and in the mirror. The mindset has three pillars: Boldness, Vision, and Empathy, backed by habits, metrics, and community. When founders treat these pillars as skills to train, the work scales from a small pilot to outcomes that touch millions.

Boldness: act, learn, raise the bar.

Boldness is disciplined risk, not theatrics. It starts with speed and ends with responsibility.

- **Ship fast, then raise quality.** Move from idea to a working pilot in weeks, not quarters. Fix the rough edges with real user feedback.
- **Place measured bets.** Keep one core bet (the product) and two smaller ones (a channel and a price point). Cap downside with clear stop-loss rules.
- **Treat compliance as a feature.** Register early, file on time, protect data, pay dues. Trust compounds when the paperwork is clean.

Field habits

- 24-hour rule for first response to every lead.
- Weekly release with one visible improvement for users.
- The founder spends five hours each week with customers, not slides.

Boldness metrics

- Time to pilot: idea to first paying user within 60–90 days.
- Conversion: at least 10 per cent of trials convert to paid in one segment before expanding.

- Unit economics: positive contribution at the smallest viable order size within six months in one city or district.

Vision: aim far, build near

Vision means holding a long horizon while solving one concrete problem today.

- **Pick a north star you can count on.** For healthcare, cost per diagnosis avoided; for skilling, days to placement; for agri, income per acre; for energy, kilowatt-hours delivered at stable voltage; for fintech, default rates at constant ticket size.
- **Design for Indian conditions.** Heat, dust, voltage fluctuation, patchy bandwidth, and multilingual use. Hardware needs serviceability. Software needs offline fallbacks.
- **Stand on public digital rails.** Use open payments, identity, data-sharing and commerce protocols to cut friction and reach towns beyond metros.
- **Blend revenue with responsibility.** Price fairly, publish service levels, honour refunds. Profit that harms trust is a dead end.

Vision metrics

- One verifiable outcome per user segment (e.g., farmer income up by a set percentage across two seasons; student pass-through to a job within a set number of days; MSME power bill down with measured uptime).
- Churn below 3–5 per cent monthly in the first steady segment.

- Net promoter score above 40 in at least one city or district before scaling.

Empathy: listen until the pattern speaks

Empathy is not a slogan. It is a method to find the real constraint and remove it.

- **Study the whole day, not only the task.** A nurse on a night shift, a driver at noon in peak heat, a teacher with a crowded class, design decisions change when you see the context.
- **Build in local languages and gestures.** Fewer screens, larger tap targets, voice input where literacy is a barrier, and helplines that pick up.
- **Price with the customer's cash cycle.** Harvest-linked for farm inputs, weekly for gig workers, semester-linked for skilling, slabbed for utilities.
- **Close the loop.** If something breaks, fix it and report back. The second response matters more than the first promise.

Empathy metrics

- Support resolution time under 24 hours for 80 per cent of tickets.
- First-contact resolution above 60 per cent within three months of launch.
- Usability score above 80 on task completion for first-time users in two languages.

A founder's operating system (India-scale)

Daily

- Review yesterday's top three user issues and the single change that addresses at least one.
- Speak to one customer, one partner, and one team member outside your direct function.

Weekly

- Publish a one-page "what shipped, what changed for the user."
- Visit the field: a ward office, a farm, a school, a clinic, a workshed, a substation, where the result happens.
- Track three numbers only: new actives, retained actives, unit contribution.

Monthly

- Audit data consent and security.
- Close books on time.
- Share a short impact note: incomes, learning outcomes, energy uptime, safety incidents prevented.

Proof that mindset scales impact

- **Jobs and skills:** Founders who align training with employer demand reduce time-to-placement dramatically and raise retention in tier-2 and tier-3 cities.

- **Health access:** Remote consults paired with low-cost diagnostics shorten travel and waiting time, and increase adherence when nudges are in the local language.
- **Farmer incomes:** Soil testing, water-efficient irrigation, and assured offtake can lift net earnings per acre, season after season, when service and finance are bundled.
- **Clean power:** Rooftop solar with smart metering for small factories lowers energy cost volatility and improves uptime when paired with maintenance SLAs.
- **Digital finance:** Instant payments, verified identity, and consented data sharing expand formal credit for small businesses, with lower fraud when risk engines are tuned to local patterns.

Community: mentors, peers, and public goods

- **Mentors**: Shorten the learning curve in pricing, hiring, finance, and sales. A few hours a month from people who have built before can save quarters of drift.
- **Peer circles**: Prevent founder isolation and bring hard feedback early.
- **Public infrastructure**: Payment rails, identity, open networks for e-commerce and data, reduces the cost of trust and discovery. Use them well, with consent and care.

Ethics as an accelerator

- Publish service levels and meet them.
- Tell customers what you collect and why, then honour their choice.
- Pay suppliers on time; many are first-generation entrepreneurs.
- File taxes and returns without delay. Clean records open doors.

The inner line that holds it all together

Boldness without empathy can bruise. Empathy without vision can drift. Vision without boldness can stall. The work sings when all three move as one. Purpose-driven founders in India already prove this in clinics and classrooms, on farms and shop floors, in small workshops and busy data centres.

Carry this mindset wherever you build: take the next step, measure what matters, keep your word, and teach what you learn. When many work this way, progress does not shout. It becomes normal. And that is how an economy grows with dignity, one reliable promise at a time.

Here's a fully human rewrite that keeps your substance, trims any machine-y edges, and flows like a closing note read aloud in a hall full of founders and students.

India's Rise Through Enterprise

Entrepreneurship is the heartbeat of India's transformation. It turns ideas into tools that people use, work into income that reaches homes, and courage into proof that change can be built with two steady hands and a clear head.

Work and growth. New ventures hire engineers, nurses, sales staff, drivers, designers, and coders; they also spark indirect work in delivery, maintenance, finance, and training. India counted more than 120,000 active startups in 2025 and well over a hundred unicorns. Together, they add meaningfully to national output and widen the circle of dignity that steady work brings. Digital rails keep momentum high. UPI clears billions of payments each month, which means a fruit seller in Madurai and a bookshop in Shillong can take money in seconds and close daybooks without fuss. Women-founded companies now form a rising share of new registrations, and each win at the founder's desk carries forward into school fees paid on time and better health choices at home.

Solutions made for Indian realities. Builders who design for heat, dust, crowded wards, patchy networks, and many languages create tools that last. Telemedicine shortens queues and saves wages lost to travel. Agri platforms link soil testing, crop advisory, and market access, helping small plots earn more per acre. Rooftop solar with smart meters trims factory bills and smooths power cuts. Skills companies tie coursework to employer demand, so a certificate leads to a first offer letter and a family's first step into formal work. Fintech uses consented data to extend small, fast credit to vendors who carry a business in a bag on a scooter.

Learning that multiplies. A founder who gives two hours a month to a younger team can change a product's fate. Indian Angel Network, NASSCOM programmes, Atal Incubation Centres, and state missions pair guidance with markets and early cheques. Public digital goods lower the cost of trust and discovery for every team, whether they write code in Kochi or fabricate parts in Rajkot. When experienced operators share how they priced, hired, complied, and survived, newer teams avoid traps and stay alive long enough to learn.

Security and resilience. Young firms now supply drones, anti-drone sensors, rugged edge computing, mapping, and secure software for forces working in tough terrain. iDEX has opened doors to prototype contracts and problem statements that matter on the ground. Local design and manufacture reduce import pain, keep sensitive know-how in the country, and build confidence that India can protect and serve with equipment made at home.

Habits that compound. The most durable gains come from culture. Pay suppliers on the date promised. Ship when you said you would. Protect user data. Treat staff with fairness during feast and famine. Publish what worked so others waste less time. Reinvest in training and research. These habits travel across districts and sectors, and they turn a collection of ventures into an ecosystem that people trust.

What the next decade can hold. With clean rules, steady institutions, and reliable public rails, the startup share of the economy can rise toward a tenth by the mid-2030s. Direct and indirect work can reach tens of millions as supply chains spread through tier-2 and tier-3 cities. Deep tech, clean energy, health, and farm services can anchor strategic autonomy. Exports from SaaS, media, design, and knowledge services can carry India's name into new markets while keeping value onshore. More women at the founder table and more youth in skilled roles will broaden leadership and lift households that have waited a long time for a fair chance.

Why it matters beyond numbers. A tool that saves a nurse ten minutes per patient changes the care a ward can give by evening. A sensor that helps a patrol see farther changes the way a family sleeps in a border village. A payment link that clears for a hawker at closing time changes a child's supper. Small wins, repeated across a vast country, become national strength.

Your part in it. If you build, build with purpose. If you have learned, teach. If you hire, train. If you earn, pay on time. If you grow, stay within the law and keep your word. Measure what your product does for the person who uses it, not only what it does for your revenue line. Count the apprentices you move into careers, the suppliers you pull into formal finance, the clinics or schools you help work better. That score tells the real story.

This is how India moves from potential to performance. One reliable promise kept. One fair price offered. One young team guided.

One hard problem solved, then another, and another, across 1.4 billion lives.

✦ ✦ ✦

6

The Mission: The India We Must Build

"A dream is not that which you see while sleeping, it is something that does not let you sleep."
– A. P. J. Abdul Kalam

The Dream of a Developed India

Every great civilisation earns its place in history through what it dares to build.

In our case, the inheritance is luminous: the zero and yoga, schools of philosophy and movements for freedom, science that reaches the Moon and Mars, a spiritual imagination that centres dignity and duty. Now the hinge turns. The moment asks for reinvention, for the courage to pair memory with bold creation, for resolve that turns vision into daily work.

A developed India begins with dignity. The measure is simple and human: a child who can read and eat well, a teenager who can learn a skill that pays, a young adult who can find work with meaning, a woman who can travel without fear, a citizen who feels that belonging is real. Strength and compassion are not rivals in this future; they stand together. Technology serves people, not the other way round. Innovation lifts productivity, and it also restores time to families and care to communities.

The world is watching an economy that now ranks among the largest on the planet, a nation with a median age under thirty, a democracy that moves money across phones in seconds, a space programme that lands where few have landed, and an energy base that adds renewable capacity each month at a steady pace. These are signals, not trophies. The destination is higher living standards across districts and castes and genders, clean air and reliable water, streets that feel safe at night, schools that set minds alight, hospitals that heal without pushing families into debt, courts and services that answer on time, and enterprises that can scale from one town to many countries.

This mission calls for precision, not rhetoric. Learning outcomes must rise each year across every block, which means teacher support, foundational literacy, and skilling that matches the work of the future. Health must move from late treatment to early prevention, with primary care that catches risk before it becomes a loss. Cities must grow with public transport, waste management, and affordable housing planned together. Farms need income security through storage, processing, irrigation that saves water, and digital links to markets that pay fairly. Industry needs power that does not fail, land that is ready, logistics that cut time, and rules that are clear. Startups require early capital, patient capital, and predictable regulation. Households need insurance that works at claim time, pensions that protect age, and digital rails that keep fraud at bay.

The good news is already visible. Digital public infrastructure brings identity, payments, and data consent to the palm. Financial inclusion reaches families that once handled only cash. Highways, freight corridors, and ports shorten travel and cut costs. Renewable energy expands each year, pairing with improvements in efficiency on the demand side. Research clusters in space, biotech, materials, and computing move from promise to product. Women's self-help groups run enterprises that steady village economies. Farmer-producer bodies bargain better. Youth in Tier-2 and Tier-3 cities build companies that sell to the world. Each strand strengthens the others.

To hold ambition and equity together, the mission needs a few anchors:

- **Learning that compounds:** Early years care, strong schools, and universities tied to research and industry, so skills and science multiply each other over a lifetime.
- **Health that protects:** Primary care within reach, diagnostics that travel, insurance that pays on time, clean air and water as non-negotiables.
- **Work that scales:** A blend of manufacturing, services, and green sectors, with logistics and power that lower costs and raise quality.
- **Homes that enable:** Housing close to jobs, public transport that runs on time, safe streets, and digital access as a utility, not a luxury.
- **Finance that includes:** Credit that reaches viable micro and small firms, savings that beat inflation, and pensions that cover informal workers.

- **Justice that delivers:** Faster resolution and digital systems that reduce friction for citizens and businesses.
- **Nature that endures:** Renewable capacity, water security through storage and reuse, and agriculture that heals soil while raising income.

None of this asks for miracles. It asks for discipline, for targets that are measured in months and quarters, for feedback that changes course when results lag, for a culture that praises problem-solvers more than speech-makers. It asks leaders in government, markets, and civil society to cooperate without seeking credit first, and to keep the long view when news cycles demand heat. It asks all of us to carry pride with humility, to care for facts, to tell the truth when a plan misses the mark, and to try again quickly.

The heart of this chapter is simple: India is everyone, and everyone is India. A mason laying tiles in Surat, a nurse on the night shift in Guwahati, a coder in Coimbatore writing a module used in three continents, a farmer in Satara who installs drip and doubles yield, a teacher in Imphal who pulls reading levels up one year at a time, a constable in Jaipur who ensures girls reach home safe, a scientist in Thiruvananthapuram who designs a lighter, stronger alloy, a craftswoman in Kutch whose design sells online to Tokyo and Toronto. This is the development model, living and breathing.

Great civilisations do not wait for permission to rise. They decide, then they build in public view, one policy, one product, one classroom, one clinic at a time. We inherit wisdom and courage in abundance. The call now is to turn them into outcomes that every family can feel.

If this is the India we must build, how do we convert national ambition into daily, measurable gains for each citizen, year after year, without leaving anyone behind?

From Survival to Significance

For years after independence the national task was clear: feed families, build core industries, connect far corners, and prove that democracy can deliver; that phase delivered the Green Revolution, a steel base from Bhilai to Bokaro, nationwide banking reach through nationalisation, and a public health and schooling network that raised life expectancy above seventy years and pushed literacy near eighty percent, so the ground under our feet is firmer than at any time in living memory.

The mission now rises to a higher plane: significance on the world stage through science, art, technology, philosophy, and public leadership, where India sets standards rather than follows them, where ideas and institutions born here travel outward with confidence and care.

A mindset of possibility must lead this phase; the country has the world's fifth-largest economy, a median age near twenty-nine, and the deepest digital rails among large nations through Aadhaar, UPI and fast data, which together move billions of authenticated payments each month and bring formal finance to households that once handled only cash, while more than one hundred unicorns, one hundred thousand plus startups, and millions of small firms turn code and craft into income in cities and districts that rarely featured in older growth stories.

Significance carries a scorecard, not slogans. Learning outcomes must rise every single year in every block; foundational reading by Class 3 becomes non-negotiable; skilling aligns with fields that create work at scale, such as electronics, mobility, green energy, deep tech and healthcare. Primary care expands screening so prevention saves lives and money; maternal and child indicators move toward the best global quartile; health insurance pays on time and without friction. Cities plan housing, transit and waste together so commutes shorten and air grows cleaner; districts strengthen cold chains and storage so farm income steadies through the year; logistics corridors cut travel time for freight to single-digit hours across major routes.

Energy and environment must pull in the same direction. Solar capacity already crosses sixty-five gigawatts, and wind stands near forty-five, with hydropower and bioenergy adding balance; green hydrogen pilots begin to clean up steel and fertiliser; efficiency gains reduce peak loads; every new megawatt sits beside a plan for storage and grid modernisation. Water security advances through groundwater recharge, river rejuvenation, drip and sprinkler coverage, and city-level reuse targets that turn wastewater into a resource.

Finance underpins the step-up. Jan Dhan accounts number in the hundreds of millions, UPI moves more transactions in a month than many card networks do in a year, and retail participation in markets grows through low-fee platforms; the next leg widens credit to women-led collectives, farmer producer bodies, and micro-enterprises with clean data trails that cut risk and cost. Pensions and insurance protect informal workers so families can plan long horizons without fear.

Culture, tourism and soft power carry their weight too. Forty-plus UNESCO sites, classical and folk traditions in every state, wellness systems that draw travellers, and a creative economy spanning cinema, crafts, design, and music generate employment while strengthening identity. When a handloom cluster in Kanchipuram sells to Seoul and Toronto, or a film from Kochi trends in Madrid, significance becomes visible far from our shores.

Governance gives the flywheel its spin. Time-bound clearances, predictable rules, fast contract enforcement, and secure digital public goods let citizens and firms move faster with fewer uncertainties; transparency and accountability keep trust high; data protection and cybersecurity guard the rails that now carry daily life.

Unity raises the ceiling on every target. Women in the workforce, equal pay for equal work, safety in streets and transport, and access to credit and property rights multiply national output; inclusion across caste, region, and language converts demographic size into collective strength; service delivery that treats every citizen with respect deepens the bond between people and state.

This is the meaning of the leap from survival to significance: a country that feeds itself well and then feeds ideas to the world, that manufactures at scale and also invents at the frontier, that honours its elders and hands a wider horizon to its young, that measures success in rupees and in dignity. The task now is to turn will into weekly progress, to track outcomes with honesty, to course-correct without delay, and to keep the focus on results that families can feel in income, safety, learning, health and pride.

India vs. India: The Battle We Must End

The hardest contest runs within our borders. It shows up when citizens fight one another instead of fighting hunger, joblessness, and lost chances. It takes shape when religion, region, caste, or political colour becomes a wall rather than a window. It grows when headlines reward anger, and we forget that the flag, the soil, and the future are shared.

A country of 1.4 billion cannot afford that drift. India stands fifth in the global economy, with a median age of twenty-nine and more than nine hundred million internet users. Digital public rails move billions of payments each month. Highways, freight corridors, ports, and airports expand year after year. These are foundations with weight. When our energy turns inward against each other, gains slow. While we argue, others build; while we split, others scale.

True competition sits outside our quarrels. It lives in higher learning outcomes, faster justice, cleaner air, cheaper logistics, deeper science, and wider opportunity than peer nations can deliver. The day we treat that as the real race, transformation gathers pace.

Start with shared goals that every district can feel: Foundational reading by Class 3 across every block. Skilling seats that match growth fields such as electronics, mobility, clean energy, materials, and health. Apprenticeships that convert training into wages. Strong primary care that catches risk early, with insurance that pays on time. Safe water and working sanitation for every school and clinic. These are not slogans. They are measurable.

Lift unity through outcomes, not rhetoric: Interstate movement of goods already accelerates under common tax rails. Push the logistics bill toward a single-digit share of GDP through better roads, rail capacity, and ports. Keep city buses frequent, metros expanding, and footpaths unbroken so women and elders can move without fear. Build more student hostels and working women's hostels near job clusters. Expand lighting, CCTV where useful, and swift case handling so safety feels real.

Turn scale into strength: A country with twenty-two official languages, twenty-eight states, and eight union territories carries a natural test of coordination. Use that diversity to pilot, learn, and copy fast. If one state halves learning gaps with simple classroom support, carry the method nationwide. If another doubles farmer's income through storage and processing, replicate the cold-chain design. Celebrate the playbook that works, not the party that claims it.

Put numbers in the national scoreboard

- Raise labour force participation for women every year, with credit, market access, and land titles supporting enterprises at the base.
- Cut court pendency with evening benches, digital case flow, and mediation centres.
- Add renewable capacity each month while pairing it with storage and smarter grids so power holds steady.
- Bring down PM2.5 in the largest cities with time-bound targets, clean buses, and stricter fuel and construction standards.

- Push learning gains in every district using independent testing and public dashboards that parents can read.

Let finance carry inclusion to the last mile: More than four-fifths of adults hold bank accounts. UPI already moves more transactions in a month than many card networks do in a year. The next leap widens formal credit to micro and small firms with clean data trails, gives pensions to informal workers, and grows affordable insurance that actually pays. Savings must beat inflation, not fear. Funds must reach a promising enterprise in Barmer as easily as one in Bengaluru.

Keep culture as a force for cohesion and jobs: Forty-plus UNESCO heritage sites, classical and folk traditions in every state, festivals that fill calendars from Kutch to Kohima, and a creative economy spanning cinema, crafts, design, music, and games. This sector heals divides while earning incomes. When a handloom cluster in Kanchipuram sells to Seoul and Toronto, or a film from Kochi trends in Madrid, pride travels where politics cannot.

Protect debate, reject hate: Strong nations argue on policy and numbers. Weak nations trade insults. Let us choose strong. Demand civility from leaders, media, and ourselves. Reward those who solve, not those who inflame. Teach digital hygiene so young citizens spot manipulative content and refuse to share it.

Build habits that end the civil cold war

- Mixed-neighbourhood schools that bring children from different backgrounds into the same room.

- National service options in health, education, and disaster response that mix youth from many states for a year of work.
- Shared cultural calendars in cities that host craft, food, and music across regions.
- Sports leagues at the district level that pull talent from every caste and community onto the same team.

Hold leaders to the same yardstick: Any party, any government, any city hall. Publish quarterly progress on schools, clinics, crime resolution, transport, jobs, pollution, and business registrations. If performance rises, keep going. If it stalls, change the method. Unity grows when fairness is visible.

The enemy is not the neighbour's faith or surname. The enemy is wasted potential. The old habit of India versus India hands victory to poverty, disease, and ignorance. End that habit, and the map begins to glow.

A nation where a mason in Surat, a nurse in Guwahati, a coder in Coimbatore, a farmer in Satara, a teacher in Imphal, a constable in Jaipur, a scientist in Thiruvananthapuram, and a craftswoman in Bhuj can each point to steady gains in income, safety, learning, and health is a nation that moves from noise to substance. That is significant.

Carry this line forward: our real contest is India with the world. Choose unity with results, and the flag stands taller in every lane.

We vs. the World: A New National Mindset

For years, our energy drained into quarrels that yielded little. The next phase demands a different stance, one team, one scoreboard, one outcome that families can feel. Call it healthy competition with the world. Call it ambition that keeps its feet on the ground. Pride in work. Confidence with proof.

This is not hostility. This is clarity. The goal is simple: lead in fields where scale, skill, and values give India a natural edge, and close gaps where delivery still lags. Think of nations that chose a single animating idea. Post-war Japan proved the force of discipline through quality. South Korea turned scarcity into design and innovation. China planned and executed at speed. India's line can be stronger: unity, democracy, and human spirit, backed by numbers that move every year.

Why does the timing favour India

- A population near 1.4 billion with a median age of around twenty-nine means two decades of workforce strength if skilling and health keep pace.
- Internet users cross nine hundred million, with the world's most affordable data and digital rails that carry identity, payments, and consent securely. UPI alone processes more than fifteen billion transfers in a typical month, linking street vendors and large firms on the same platform.
- Renewable power keeps expanding, with solar capacity above sixty-five gigawatts and wind near forty-five. Hydropower and bioenergy provide balance.

- A startup base above one hundred thousand firms, more than one hundred unicorns, and SaaS players that sell worldwide signal a deepening technology engine.
- Highways, dedicated freight corridors, new airports, and faster ports keep cutting logistics time, which lowers costs for every sector.

These are not decorations. They are levers that can shift national outcomes if we use them with purpose.

What a "We vs. the World" mindset looks like in practice

1) Treat learning as the first competitive advantage

Foundational literacy by Class 3 in every block, year-on-year gains measured openly, and skilling that matches demand in electronics, mobility, clean energy, health services, advanced materials, and computing. Apprenticeships that move straight into wages. Teacher mentoring that raises classroom craft. Scholarships that follow the student, with outcomes tracked.

2) Build a healthy base that protects growth

Primary care close to home, diagnostics that travel, insurance that pays on time, and public health data that triggers prevention early. Maternal and child indicators must push into the top global quartile. Air and water standards are enforced, so chronic disease falls, saving both lives and money.

3) Make industry faster, cleaner, and larger

Plug-and-play industrial land with power that holds steady, single-window clearances that truly finish within weeks, and logistics that move freight across major routes in single-digit hours. Pair renewable capacity with storage and smart grids so factories run without interruption. Electronics, semiconductors, green steel, chemicals, defence, and pharmaceuticals can each carry millions of jobs if inputs and approvals stay predictable.

4) Turn farms into value creators

Irrigation that saves water, soil health restored, storage and cold chains that cut losses, processing that raises price realisation, and digital markets that widen buyers. Farmer producer bodies and women's groups are linked to working capital at fair rates. Rural broadband, plus solar pumps, plus local processing equals income that holds steady through the year.

5) Let finance include and accelerate

More than four-fifths of adults hold bank accounts. UPI spans the nation. The next step is clean credit for micro and small firms, pensions for informal workers, and affordable insurance that pays without friction. Retail participation in markets keeps deepening through low-fee platforms. Capital must reach a promising enterprise in Barmer as easily as one in Bengaluru.

6) Back creators and soft power

Over forty UNESCO sites, classical and folk traditions in every state, a film industry that speaks many languages, crafts that employ millions, and a digital audience on a global scale. Culture heals divides and earns income. When a weaver in Kanchipuram sells to Seoul, when music from Shillong trends in Berlin, soft power compounds.

7) Keep governance on a clock

Time-bound clearances, e-courts that reduce pendency, open data that lets citizens verify delivery, and cybersecurity that protects the public rails. Rules that are clear help firms plan and help families trust the state.

A shared scorecard that lifts pride and performance

- **Learning:** Every district posts annual gains in reading and numeracy.
- **Health:** primary care coverage expands, out-of-pocket spending falls, and claim settlement times shrink.
- **Jobs:** labour force participation for women rises each year, with credit and markets linked to their enterprises.
- **Air and water:** PM2.5 falls in the largest cities, wastewater reuse targets grow, and groundwater recharge improves.
- **Power:** renewable capacity rises monthly, storage projects come online, and outages decline.
- **Courts and services:** case disposal rates improve, service delivery deadlines are met.
- **Logistics:** turnaround times at ports and freight corridors keep dropping.

Publish the numbers quarterly. Celebrate what works. Fix what stalls. Copy fast across states without pride of authorship.

The mindset shift in one sentence

Stop asking whether we can. Start declaring where and when we will. A nation that speaks with one voice on outcomes gathers speed. A mason in Surat, a nurse in Guwahati, a coder in Coimbatore, a farmer in Satara, a teacher in Imphal, a constable in Jaipur, a scientist in Thiruvananthapuram, a craftswoman in Bhuj, each one moves with the same intent: build, improve, include.

If 1.4 billion citizens channel effort into making, healing, learning, and serving, catching up ceases to be the frame. The world begins to follow our lead.

The Role of Government: Spreading Unity and Patriotism

A nation moves fastest when policy travels with purpose. Laws, budgets, and projects matter, yet the spirit that binds citizens matters as much. Public institutions can set that spirit. They can lift conduct in daily life, teach pride without prejudice, and make service a habit.

What patriotism looks like in daily life

Patriotism shows up when a citizen keeps a promise, treats a neighbour with respect, pays taxes on time, keeps the street clean, stands up for a girl on a bus, mentors a student, and volunteers during floods or drought. Government can turn these private acts into a public norm through steady, visible programs that reward integrity, cooperation, and contribution.

Lessons from what already works

- **Civic campaigns that built shared effort:** Swachh Bharat turned sanitation into a dinner-table conversation and helped rural India approach near-universal toilet coverage, which improved dignity and health.
- **Pairing cultures across states:** Ek Bharat Shreshtha Bharat twinned states for language, food, and festivals and showed how curiosity reduces prejudice.
- **Youth service at scale:** National Service Scheme units in schools and colleges place students in health drives, literacy support, and disaster response. Nehru Yuva Kendras energise village youth clubs for sports, culture, and community work.
- **Mass participation days:** Yoga Day events, Fit India runs, and cleanliness drives created quick, repeatable rituals that make citizens feel part of something larger.

These efforts point to a simple truth. When the State offers clear goals, easy ways to join, and visible recognition, participation rises across age, caste, faith, and region.

"One India, One Dream": a unifying civic programme

A national umbrella with local roots can turn unity into routine.

Core pillars

1. **Unity Days in every school and college**

   Monthly projects that mix students across communities. Examples: joint reading camps in slums, heritage clean-ups, traffic safety marshals near schools, tree-planting with survival audits after six months.

   One paired language activity each term, so children sing, cook, or recite from a partner state.

2. **Workplace Service Weeks**

   Public and private employers adopt a ward, lake, or school cluster for the year.

   Staff contribute skills: accountants help SHGs with bookkeeping, engineers audit road safety, and designers upgrade signage in government hospitals.

3. **Neighbourhood Honour Roll**

   Local administrations publish a simple monthly list: the mohalla that kept waste segregation highest, the village that achieved 100 per cent immunisation on time, the bus depot with zero harassment complaints, and the police station with the fastest response in its class.

4. **National Storybank**

   Public broadcasters and private platforms curate short films, podcasts, and reels that spotlight citizens who served beyond identity lines. Selection focuses on verifiable outcomes, not celebrity.

5. **Service as a rite of passage**

   A voluntary one-year Young India Service Track after Class 12 or graduation, with placements in primary care, school tutoring, irrigation maintenance, and disaster readiness. Stipends, skill certificates, and college credit create strong uptake.

6. **Diaspora Bridge**

   Overseas Indians mentor startups from districts, sponsor school libraries, and fund clean-water projects. District authorities host quarterly virtual demo days that match needs with support.

Make it measurable

Unity grows when progress is visible. A public dashboard at the district level can track:

- **Participation**: share of schools holding Unity Days each month, students and employees logged in service hours, SHGs and FPOs mentored.
- **Safety and respect**: time to register and resolve harassment complaints on public transport, number of mixed-community events held without incident.
- **Cleanliness and health**: segregated waste share, open defecation reversion checks, immunisation timeliness, TB detection and treatment success.
- **Education and skill**: attendance recovery after holidays, reading gains in Classes 2–3, apprenticeship seats filled, completion and job placement.
- **Environment**: tree survival rates after six and twelve months, waterbody revival milestones, air-quality days in safe bands.

Targets sit in quarters and years, not speeches. Districts that hit goals receive untied funds for local priorities and public recognition ceremonies where the credit names teams, not parties.

Build emotional infrastructure

Physical infrastructure gives roads and power. Emotional infrastructure gives trust.

- **Shared symbols with shared conduct:** Flag days are tied to verified community work, not rallies. Anthem mornings in offices during Service Weeks, followed by one hour of problem-solving for the adopted ward.
- **Common calendars:** A simple, nationally shared sequence: January literacy sprints, April water harvesting, July tree care checks, October cleanliness, December kindness drives for the elderly and the homeless.
- **Curriculum threads:** Age-appropriate civic content: consent and gender respect in middle school, digital hygiene and fact-checking in secondary school, financial literacy and local governance in college.
- **Sport as a bridge:** District leagues with mixed teams selected through open trials, not patronage. Matches rotate across schools, ITIs, and colleges to spread pride.

Guardrails that keep unity genuine

- **Non-partisan voice:** Campaigns carry the Republic's insignia and local institutions' names. They do not carry individual leaders' faces.

- **Inclusion by design:** Committees balance gender, caste, and region. Announcements appear in local languages. Accessibility standards cover ramps, captions, and sign language.
- **Dignity first:** No shaming. Recognition goes to effort and outcomes. Complaints have clear, safe channels, and responses are time-bound.
- **Data privacy:** Consent layers protect participants. Dashboards show aggregates, not personal details.

Funding the effort

- **Three-way model:** Central seed grants set standards. States co-fund and adapt. CSR and philanthropy underwrite content, technology, and last-mile costs.
- **Micro-grants that travel fast:** Schools, youth clubs, RWAs, SHGs, and FPOs receive small, outcome-linked grants with simple audits.
- **Frugal tech:** Use existing digital rails for attendance, task lists, and recognition badges. Open APIs let startups build local apps in Indian languages.

What success feels like

A Class 3 child reads at grade level and spends one morning collaborating with students from all religions and regions on a community project. A woman can ride home at nine in the evening because lighting, patrols, and quick case handling are routine. A farmer sells produce through a local FPO and sees payments hit the bank the same day. A bus conductor treats every passenger with courtesy because training, monitoring, and rewards align. A street in a mixed neighbourhood celebrates a cleanliness milestone with music and food from many kitchens. Each scene is small. Together, they form the national character.

The call

Unity is not a slogan, and patriotism is not a single day. Both grow from repeated acts that become custom. Government can lead with steady programmes, clear numbers, and fair recognition. Citizens can respond with time, skill, and grace. When that partnership hardens into habit, the flag is carried in conduct, the anthem is carried in service, and the nation walks taller in every lane.

The Role of Citizens: Building, Not Blaming

A developed nation grows when people decide that progress is personal. The government lays rails, yet trains move because citizens bring fuel, time, and will. Every household, every lane, every ward can tilt the story either towards excuse or towards effort, and the difference shows up in numbers that tell a plain tale of participation.

When public services falter, apathy deepens the dent. Accountability begins with citizens who record an issue, track the remedy, and follow through until the final coat of paint dries, which is why India's information laws matter as everyday tools rather than lofty promises, and why filings under the Right to Information framework continue across ministries and states year after year, creating a public record that pushes officials to answer with facts rather than opinion.

Democracy asks for more than opinions; it asks for turnout. The Election Commission's statistical reports confirm that national participation has held strong across recent cycles, with gender gaps narrowing and several regions crossing their best figures in decades, a reminder that when citizens show up together, policy follows the pulse of real life rather than the noise of narrow echo chambers.

Financial inclusion is another arena where citizen action has moved the needle. Families who once kept savings in tins now hold accounts that receive benefits directly and transact in seconds on a phone, which is how a programme like Jan Dhan shifted from a target on paper to crores of opened accounts in practice, and why fresh enrolments keep being reported during saturation drives at the district level.

Digital payments tell the same story of ordinary people driving national efficiency. The UPI rail carries billions of transactions a month, and during festival peaks, it has crossed the 20-billion mark in a single month, cutting cash friction for street vendors, delivery workers, parent-teacher associations, and micro-enterprises that now settle dues with a scan rather than a queue.

Public health and dignity improve when citizens partner with schemes rather than watch them from afar. Rural sanitation tracking under the Swachh Bharat Mission is published as living data, visible down to the gram panchayat, which means communities can verify what is complete, what is pending, and where resources must move next. This transparency gives village councils and citizen groups the confidence to ask pointed questions and then to organise action days that finish the work.

The same civic spirit can guide daily conduct in ways that never make headlines yet change outcomes. Residents' associations that sort waste and monitor water meters reduce municipal strain. Parent groups that volunteer reading hours lift learning outcomes more reliably than complaint threads. Local trade bodies that publish payment timelines improve trust across supply chains. Start-ups that mentor in government schools seed employability where it counts.

This is the mindset India needs to scale: record issues with evidence rather than rumours; use statutory tools before outrage; volunteer hours alongside funds; pay taxes on time; support local enterprises that create honest work; vote regularly and help neighbours reach the booth; keep a ledger for every public promise and every delivered result. These are simple acts, yet done at a population scale, they harden soft spots in the state, and they do it faster than any single policy can.

A citizen's oath can read like this: I will raise a ticket before I raise my voice; I will measure outcomes before I forward claims; I will mentor one learner, support one artisan, and plant one idea in my mohalla that did not exist last season. If a streetlight fails, I will log it and follow the service order to closure. If a contract seems wasteful, I will file an RTI and share the answer. If a rumour polarises the lane, I will reach out across the line and bring the conversation back to water supply, school hours, and clinic stock.

Nations grow on such habits. Policies remain words until citizens turn them into daily practice. India has already shown what happens when large numbers move together, from opening bank accounts to adopting digital payments at a scale that few believed possible, from standing in long lines to vote to checking programme dashboards for sanitation progress. The path ahead asks more of the same energy, directed with care and consistency, so that every problem that touches a home meets a citizen who is willing to build rather than blame.

The Power of Emotional Patriotism

India endured centuries of invasion, colonisation, and extraction because hearts held firm when fortunes did not. That same inner strength can power the next stage of growth, turning feeling into effort and pride into daily practice.

Patriotism lives in informed devotion. It shows when a parent helps a child read, when neighbours keep a lane clean, when a trader files returns on time, and when a citizen follows the law even when no one is watching. Each small act strengthens trust, trims waste, and frees public money for schools, clinics, and roads. The spirit is national, the work is local.

Every day, patriots deserve the spotlight. Think of a teacher who lifts her classroom one lesson at a time, a farmer who shifts to soil-friendly methods and saves water each season, an entrepreneur who keeps salaries regular and adds two new jobs before the year ends, a scientist who files a patent that solves an Indian problem at Indian cost. These citizens carry the tricolour through conduct. Their wins compound quietly across districts until outcomes change.

Emotional patriotism needs form as well as feeling. Here is a simple frame any family or workplace can use.

1) Learn and serve each month

One hour a week for skill-sharing: reading circles for Classes 2-3, basic accounting for self-help groups, and digital safety for seniors. Keep a log. Track who came, what improved, and what needs attention next.

2) Keep money honest

Pay taxes on time. Prefer UPI or other traceable modes for wages and purchases. Ask for bills. These habits reduce leakage, speed refunds, and build a credit history that helps a young business borrow at a fair rate.

3) Protect shared spaces

Segregate waste at source. Report broken streetlights, potholes, and leaks through official apps and follow the ticket to closure. Plant in the monsoon and check survival after six and twelve months. Pride grows when a ward sees progress on a board, not only in a speech.

4) Respect women and children, everywhere

Intervene safely when harassment occurs. Demand lighting near bus stops and CCTV where the law requires it. Support time-bound grievance redressal at depots, campuses, and markets. A safe commute unlocks education and income for half the nation.

5) Buy Indian with standards

Choose local goods that meet quality norms. Rate service fairly. Share feedback that helps a shop or start-up improve. Commerce becomes stronger when every buyer acts like a partner in progress.

6) Vote, volunteer, verify

Help neighbours reach the booth. Read official dashboards for health, education, and sanitation before forwarding claims. File information requests when something looks off. Praise delivery that meets time and cost. Question what drifts.

7) Carry kindness into conflict

When a lane divides on faith or language, bring the talk back to water timings, clinic stock, bus frequency, and school hours. Work together on something concrete. Shared effort dissolves heat faster than argument.

Emotional patriotism turns into results when it is regular, measured, and shared. Families can set three household pledges for the year. Schools can mark one Unity Day each month with mixed-group projects. Offices can adopt a ward, a lake, or a school cluster and publish outcomes each quarter. Resident bodies can set simple targets: fewer missed waste pickups, more working streetlights, better water pressure at peak hours. Celebrate gains, correct misses, repeat the cycle.

Let the nation carry a new definition into the century. Patriotism is a steady contribution grounded in truth. It honours the flag through action more than display, through care more than noise. When millions live that meaning, India moves from sentiment to strength, from feeling to fulfilment, and from promise to proof.

The Media and the Message

The media shapes the weather in a nation's mind. In a noisy age, that duty is heavier than ratings and trends. India needs narrators who lift the horizon, not only messengers who relay conflict.

The scale is vast. India has **1,48,000+ registered periodicals** on the rolls of the Press Registrar General; the latest "Press in India" report notes **1,48,363 registered periodicals** as of March 2023, with tens of thousands filing annual statements that map languages, districts, and reach.

Television news also runs broad and deep, with government disclosures noting **nearly 400 licensed news channels** and **thousands of digital news publishers** now in the mix.

On the demand side, the digital public is immense. India is on course for **900 million+ internet users** around 2025, and news habits mirror that shift: the Reuters Institute's 2024 survey shows Indians drawing heavily on **YouTube** and **WhatsApp** for news, alongside legacy outlets. This reach can do more than relay outrage. It can set a national tone where effort is admired, integrity is normal, and public spirit feels modern, not old-fashioned.

What credible, constructive media looks like

1) Balance the rundown: For every hour of high-temperature debate, reserve a clear slot for **solution reporting**: new irrigation methods that save water in Marathwada, a low-cost air-quality fix trialled by a district school, a startup that cut hospital queue times in Ranchi. India's mix of **393 news channels** and a booming digital field gives room for formats that reward outcomes instead of volume.

2) Put the citizen maker on air: Run a weekly "**Nation Builder of the Week**" across TV, radio, print, and portals. One teacher who lifted class reading scores, one sarpanch whose panchayat met all learning hours, one lab team that open-sourced a frugal device. With **900M+ internet users** and strong video habits, these segments travel quickly across YouTube and short-video platforms.

3) Give rural news its front row: Grass-roots newsrooms already show the path. Women-led Khabar Lahariya built a reporting network across Bundelkhand and proved that coverage of roads, ration, and safety can move institutions when it stays on story and on record. Feature one such rural or district newsroom each week; link their proofs, not only their pain.

4) Track progress with the same energy as a scandal: When a city pledges to reopen lakes or a ministry commits to skill targets, build **progress dashboards** that stay on a fixed page and in a recurring TV graphic. Reference official baselines from the **Press Registrar's** public reports and other audited sources; update fortnightly so audiences see movement rather than memory.

5) Raise media literacy on air: A brief explainer segment inside prime bulletins, how to read a chart, how surveys work, what "margin of error" means, arm viewers for a world where half the country meets news on platforms first. The 2024 data confirm rising platform reliance; the answer is not alarm, it is education.

6) Showcase India's creators, not only its conflicts: From streaming to cinema, Indian screens reach hundreds of millions each week. National networks can place a steady spotlight on labs, libraries, film schools, craft clusters, and youth science fairs. Even market stories can serve this end: coverage of broadcaster reach, mergers, and audience shifts signals where attention flows and where cultural power sits.

Why this matters now

- **Reach has multiplied:** with hundreds of TV news licences and **thousands** of digital publishers, a single editorial choice can ripple across languages and districts in a day.
- **Audiences live online:** India is moving toward **900M+ internet users**; YouTube and WhatsApp are core news gateways. Responsible storytelling on these pipes sets norms for civility and shared purpose.
- **Local proof changes behaviour:** district-level reporting networks such as Khabar Lahariya show that persistent, documented coverage moves officials and budgets. Scale that practice, and the national mood shifts from complaint to completion.

A simple pledge for editors and producers

- One guaranteed solutions block per bulletin.
- One citizen maker every week.
- One rural or small-city newsroom in rotation.
- One progress dashboard that never goes off-air.
- One media-literacy minute inside prime time.

When the media keeps faith with these habits, the public square clears. People see their own effort reflected back. Leaders feel watched for outcomes, not catchphrases. The country learns to applaud tangible work as readily as theatrical speech.

Hope grows when it is verified. Give the nation facts that breathe, faces that build, and follow-ups that close the loop. That is how the message becomes a movement.

The Youth: Architects of Unity

India's young citizens carry an unusual responsibility. Their choices shape not only careers and markets, but also the tone of our democracy and the ties that hold a billion people together. The numbers alone tell a story of scale and promise. Government data places youth at more than a quarter of the population, with India holding the world's largest youth cohort; the median age remains under thirty, which means the country still has time to turn energy into lasting capability.

Digital reach multiplies that promise. Reports through 2025 show India crossing nine hundred million internet users, with the majority growth outside metros, and a social-media-savvy generation that builds movements in hours, not months. This reach is not a vanity metric; it is the plumbing for civic drives, local entrepreneurship, peer learning, and rapid skill sharing.

The scaffolding for youth leadership already exists; it needs scale and steady encouragement. The Nehru Yuva Kendra Sangathan counts around 8.5 million enrolled youth across more than three lakh clubs, present in nearly every district. The National Service Scheme remains one of the country's largest student movements and continues to expand its volunteer base through national festivals and state drives. These networks train habits that a society needs every day: showing up, solving together, staying with a task until a lane is clean, a village is vaccinated, a riverbank is replanted.

Innovation is not confined to elite labs. Atal Tinkering Labs are now in ten thousand schools, with more than one crore students using low-cost tools to prototype solutions, guided by thousands of volunteer mentors. Link that to the Skill India pipeline, which has trained more than sixteen million candidates under PMKVY since 2015, and you begin to see a ladder from curiosity to employability that reaches deep into smaller towns.

Entrepreneurship is no longer a side story. As of mid-2025, more than 1.8 lakh startups are recognised by DPIIT. Many are founded in Tier-2 and Tier-3 cities, and many sell outside India from day one. When young founders build products for farmers, clinics, classrooms, and local shops, they do more than raise capital; they normalise cooperation across language and region, and they pull talent home.

Unity grows when young people turn scale into service. Here is a practical frame that keeps the spirit high and the feet on the ground:

- **Learn, then teach:** Join an ATL, a campus innovation cell, or an online cohort, then run a weekend club for school students in your mohalla. One trained volunteer often unlocks dozens of learners.
- **Build in public:** Use open source, share roadmaps in local languages, and keep progress transparent.

Public builds earn trust across communities and lower the barrier for the next team to start.

- **Adopt a problem, not a headline:** Water logging around a station, low enrolment in a government school, smoke from seasonal burning near fields; choose one, map stakeholders, and design a monthly sprint.
- **Use the rails that already work:** UPI for micro-donations, district NYKS/NSS offices for volunteers, PMKVY partners for training rooms, and college maker spaces for prototypes.
- **Measure what matters:** Hours taught, trees that survived the summer, girls who returned to school and stayed, shopkeepers who adopted digital receipts; report these numbers locally and often.

Culture travels fastest when youth carry it. A coder mentoring schoolgirls on basic AI ethics, a nursing student running a monthly anaemia camp, a design graduate documenting local craft techniques for a co-op website, a group of trainees fixing a panchayat office's record-keeping with a simple spreadsheet; these are not small things. They cool tempers and grow confidence. They create the memory of working side by side.

The country already rewards such work with platforms and reach. OTT audiences have crossed six hundred million, and social tools spotlight positive stories when creators choose responsibly. When youth teams tell the story of a restored lake, a zero-waste festival, or a village becoming fully digital, they make unity visible and attractive.

A final ask, simple and firm. Pick one role this year and stay with it: NSS or NYKS volunteer, ATL mentor, startup founder solving a local pain point, PMKVY trainee who returns as a trainer, student reporter tracking civic outcomes in your ward. The nation does not move on speeches; it moves on calendars and checklists that a million young hands agree to keep.

India's youth will be known by three habits: learning that never stops, service that asks for no spotlight, and invention that includes the last home in the last lane. Keep those habits, and the flag looks less like a symbol and more like a promise kept.

The Power of One

History keeps a quiet record of how one life can tilt a continent. Mohandas K. Gandhi showed the people that truth and restraint could move empires, from Champaran in 1917 to the Salt March in 1930 and the Quit India call of 1942. Dr A. P. J. Abdul Kalam took a village child's curiosity to ISRO and DRDO, helped advance India's space and defence programmes, and, as President from 2002 to 2007, turned science into a language that schoolchildren could trust. Mother Teresa built a community of service that reached the sick and the abandoned, earned the Nobel Peace Prize in 1979, and taught that care begins with the person in front of you.

Their tools differed, their temperaments differed, their fields differed. What joined them was an unwillingness to wait.

Each citizen carries a similar spark. It grows when thought turns into effort, and effort turns into habit. The decision might look small on the day it is taken: mentoring two students after class, filing a civic complaint and staying with it to closure, setting up a neighbourhood blood-donor list, standardising wages in a small workshop, publishing a clear set of accounts for a community fund, planting trees in the monsoon and checking survival through the summer, learning a new skill and teaching it forward. Small steps gather witnesses. Witnesses become partners.

Ask one plain question and answer it with your calendar: "Am I waiting for someone else to build the India I dream of, or am I willing to start today?"

Change often begins with a single household decision. A handful of neighbours who copy it turn effort into a pattern. A hundred who keep at it turn the pattern into a norm that others begin to expect. That is how a lane gets safer, a school improves attendance, a clinic meets its hours, a ward cleans a lake, a city learns to separate waste, a district keeps girls in secondary school, and a country learns to believe in its own work.

One hand sets the pace. Ten who follow create momentum. A hundred who persist change the outcome.

The Vision Ahead

"The future depends on what we do in the present." – Mahatma Gandhi

The India we must build will not follow another country's script. It will be an India that grows in its own language, blending ancient learning with modern invention, freedom with fairness, democracy with discipline. The world has seen nations rise through wealth or war; India will rise through wisdom.

True progress here will be measured not by how many towers reach the sky, but by how many lives rise with them. Our strength is in people, **1.4 billion citizens**, most under the age of thirty. By **2035**, nearly **800 million** will belong to the middle class, forming the largest working-age population on Earth. When such energy finds direction, the result is not growth alone, but renewal.

This new India will lead with conscience. Economic power matters, but moral example matters more. We are already proving that development and inclusion can go together. Over **80% of Indian adults now have bank accounts**, **UPI handles over 15 billion transactions each month**, and nearly **900 million people are online**. These are not just statistics; they are signs of access, of opportunity touching villages that once stood apart.

Progress cannot come at the cost of heritage. Our **22 official languages**, **1,600 dialects**, and **dozens of UNESCO heritage sites** remind the world that culture is not an obstacle to modernity; it is its foundation. The future classroom in India might see a girl in Manipur coding in her mother tongue, while a craftsman in Kutch sells handmade textiles to a buyer in Europe using a digital wallet. The same soil that raised poets and philosophers is now raising engineers, scientists, and designers who carry both tradition and technology in their hands.

When the tricolour flies each August, it should not feel like a ceremony. It should feel like routine pride, in clean streets, in honest work, in schools that teach both excellence and empathy. Every honest act of service, every product made with integrity, is another thread in that flag.

This is not a dream of someday. It is a plan already unfolding. India is set to become the **third-largest economy by 2030**, a global leader in **renewable energy**, **biotech**, and **digital transformation**. Yet the truest success will not be in ranking charts; it will be in proving that growth can be kind, and ambition can coexist with care.

When **1.4 billion Indians** work with shared purpose, farmers, teachers, coders, artists, scientists, soldiers, and nurses, the collective effort becomes unstoppable. No global power can match a nation whose citizens move with unity and pride.

The time has come to choose: not between the past and the future, but between hesitation and belief. Because the India we must build is already within us, waiting to be lived, one act of courage at a time.

✦ ✦ ✦

EPILOGUE

THE INDIA WE CHOOSE TO BUILD

"Kaal kare so aaj kar, aaj kare so ab." Kabir's line lands like a bell. What you plan for tomorrow, do today. What you plan today, do now.

India has dreamed long enough. Vision must meet action. Every day of delay costs talent, ideas, and enterprise. The work before us is practical, urgent, and shared. The movement begins when people become builders, innovators, and leaders where they stand.

The ground we stand on

Progress rests on three pillars that rise together: dignity, reach, and fairness.

Dignity means people feel seen.

Reach means services arrive where they should.

Fairness means rules stay the same for all.

When these stand in line, a country grows without needing slogans.

Unity is the first pillar of speed. Internal quarrels slow the nation. Unity does not erase differences. It channels them into common results. Think of communities that modernise a village together. Think of states that share working models instead of trading taunts. Think of citizens who debate with care and never shake the country's integrity. A national message, India First: Unity in Action, can move through schools, offices, and factories so that patriotism becomes daily conduct, not ceremony.

Leadership in every lane

Leadership no longer sits only in a ministry or a corner office. It shows up in villages through water management, smart farming, and strong schools. It shows up in cities through entrepreneurs who build clean industries and create jobs. It shows up in institutions through teachers, doctors, and engineers who lift the next generation. When leadership becomes a habit for 1.4 billion people, momentum becomes natural.

Knowledge and skill as tools

Scale is an advantage when minds are ready. Skill hubs in every district, incubators for young problem-solvers, and community mentorships can convert a youth wave into a talent wave. Curricula must link to work, research, and ethics. The goal is simple: move from rote to problem-solving and from certificates to competence.

Citizenship that builds

A movement fails without mass participation. Action speaks through clean streets, protected lakes, careful use of water, time given in schools and clinics, and steady work in local councils. Digital platforms can help citizens track budgets, propose ideas, and vote on priorities. The mantra is clear: lead where you are.

Clean governance and trust

Corruption wastes years. Digital processes that reduce discretion, firm action against fraud, safety for whistleblowers, and rewards for service excellence can rebuild trust. Governance must move from file-pushing to outcomes. When institutions earn trust, investment and effort follow.

Enterprise for jobs and confidence

Enterprise lifts confidence across a country. Rural ventures in farm-tech, clean energy, and crafts can raise incomes. Urban ventures in fintech, AI, biotech and green industry can raise exports. Credit lines that reach first-time founders, microfinance that respects borrowers, and venture funds that back patient innovation will widen the base. Enterprise does more than raise GDP. It raises self-belief.

Technology with care for the earth

Growth without care harms the very ground that feeds it. Solar, wind, and storage need scale in every state. Smart transport, efficient buildings, and water-saving systems reduce waste. Digital literacy must reach every household so people can work, learn, and trade with confidence. India can prove that technology and stewardship can move together.

A healthy ambition: We and the world

The mindset for the next phase is simple: compete with the best on earth. Let sport, science, arts, and industry reach world standards. National projects in space, AI, and biotech can become symbols of shared capacity.

Youth energy should flow into creation, not conflict. This is how pride turns into performance.

Media that lifts the national mood

Information shapes attention. Media can spotlight citizens who build, schools that improve, hospitals that innovate, and teams that solve. Features on nation builders, reports on solutions, and coverage of global wins by Indians can steady the public mind. When media lifts sightlines, people reach higher.

Proof that scale begins small

Three cases remind us how local action scales.

- Amul shows how farmers, through a cooperative, built a global dairy brand.
- Digital classrooms in Chhattisgarh show how rural schools can plug into world-standard lessons.
- Selco shows how solar solutions reach homes that the grid missed.

These are not headlines for a day. They have been around for a decade.

How we measure progress

Progress must be visible. Rising literacy, wider skill coverage, higher female work participation, more village and city projects, lower leakages, better nutrition and fitness, cleaner air and water, more patents, stronger results in sport, arts, and diplomacy. When people can see the numbers and feel the change, participation grows.

The inner call

Before a flag climbs a pole, a yes rises within. A yes to keep time, keep word, and keep faith with one another. Unity in practice looks ordinary and powerful at once. A maker finishes to specification and ships on schedule. A buyer pays on the date and sends thanks. A nurse learns a procedure and applies it with care. A driver stays in the lane and on time. A founder trains teams and pays on time. A veteran opens doors for the young. A voter notes promises and checks outcomes with calm.

This is the language of nationhood: keep your promise, treat people with respect, set a date and meet it, learn something new each year, teach someone each month, refuse harmful shortcuts, ask for receipts and give them, vote with memory, and work between elections. Lift the flag in your heart each morning and let your choices show it.

Patriotism need not be loud. It is patient strength. It smiles at a stranger, helps without a camera, pays bills on time, says sorry when wrong, and returns to work the next morning. Love for the country lives in deeds.

Unity is not sameness. Many voices can move in one direction. Speak freely, argue fairly, decide, and give the decision a chance. Care for those who disagree. Protect the weak. Honour builders. Celebrate those who serve without seeking applause. The world watches how we treat one another. That is our true signal.

Every sector matters. Builders, farmers, teachers, nurses, coders, artists, drivers, soldiers, traders, researchers, officers. Each carries a piece of the promise. None is spare. When any group rises, the whole rises.

The call to every Indian

The movement asks for action now. Educators, prepare minds for a wide world. Youth, innovate with courage and care. Farmers, use methods that protect soil and water. Entrepreneurs, create work and pay on time. Citizens, fight corruption with honesty and vigilance. Mentors, guide with kindness. Families, raise the young to love the country and respect work.

The India we build will be unified in purpose, strong in innovation, steady in stewardship, and admired for ethics and courage. The country will compete with the world and also set new standards for civilization by proving that unity, clear vision, and daily action create uncommon results.

The method is clear: vision joined to skill, action joined to patriotism. The responsibility is shared: every citizen, every institution, every leader. The moment is now.

United we stand as a developed India. Divided, we fall short of our gift. We have the people. We have the talent. We have the tools. We carry the memory of those who built before us and friends across the world who believe in our rise. The path is open.

When our children ask what we did, let the answer be, **We kept our word. We worked hard. We loved India in deeds. We treated one another with respect. We believed in this country and behaved like citizens of the India we wished to see.**

That will be enough. That will be victory.

Satyameva Jayate.

✦ ✦ ✦

About the Author

Shafi Shoukath is an Indian author, entrepreneur, startup founder, TEDx speaker, changemaker, and philanthropist who believes that real change begins when people take action.

He is the founder of World of IQue, a private, purpose-driven platform that backs entrepreneurs solving real Indian problems. He is also the man behind building India's first Startup Park in Bengaluru, an initiative aimed at creating a dynamic ecosystem for aspiring founders to learn, build, and scale their ideas.

The effort is simple in design and firm in intent: to help ideas grow into institutions that serve people and endure.

Through his work, Shafi brings together founders, mentors, and communities, ensuring that innovation translates into livelihoods, learning, and dignity. He strongly believes that India can move from developing to developed when vision meets disciplined execution and meaningful collaboration.

With this book, he aims to ignite a practical sense of purpose in readers who aspire to build. Dreamers, doers, and believers will find an invitation here: take responsibility, create value, and contribute to India's rise–now.

✦ ✦ ✦

www.ingramcontent.com/pod-product-compliance
Lightning Source LLC
LaVergne TN
LVHW100259210926
848480LV00003B/972
* 9 7 9 8 9 0 1 1 2 3 7 4 4 *